PROVENCAL *Interiors*

PROVENCAL
Interiors

FRENCH COUNTRY STYLE IN AMERICA

BETTY LOU PHILLIPS, ASID
PHOTOGRAPHY BY DAN PIASSICK

GIBBS·SMITH
PUBLISHER

Salt Lake City

Endsheet: American fabric house Travers

Photograph Title Page: Paying tribute to the French indoor-outdoor way of life, this conservatory opens onto a terrace ideal for alfresco dining and for entertaining an ever-expanding circle of friends. Garden views invite the outside in to a room filled with lush foliage. Glazed walls suggest age, along with the birdcages and chandelier, which are both remnants of the past. Salvaged architectural elements further lend a sophisticated note.

Photograph Contents Page: Fine bed linens—painstakingly pressed, evenly stacked, and carefully rolled—are stored in an admirable eighteenth-century Louis XV armoire. Upholstered shelves prevent these precious possessions—some old, some nearly new, most distinctly Italian—from snagging. For many centuries, towering armoires housed bridal trousseaus. Later, they guarded the family secrets. With strapping iron locks and hesitant keys, they now serve in boundless capacities.

Copyright © 1998 by Betty Lou Phillips

01 00 99 7 6 5 4

Published by
Gibbs Smith, Publisher
P.O. Box 667
Layton, Utah 84041
Orders (1-800)748-5439
Visit our web site at www.gibbs-smith.com

Designed by Traci O'Very Covey
Edited by Gail Yngve

Printed and bound by Codra Enterprises, Inc.(Carson, CA) in Korea.

Library of Congress Cataloging-in-Publication Data

Phillips, Betty Lou.
Provençal interiors / Betty Lou Phillips.
p. cm.
ISBN 0-87905-848-X
1. Interior decoration—United States—History—20th century.
2. Decoration and ornament, Rustic—France—Influence. I. Title.
NK2004.P55   1998
747.213—dc21   98-17493
                        CIP

Contents

I am grateful to the interior designers who allowed us to photograph their work, including Diane Chapman, Cheryl Driver, Charles Faudree, Bruce Foreman, Muriel Hebert, Katherine Hill, Janet Hodges, Constance Noah, Gloria Nicoud, Christina Phillips, Marilyn Phillips, Richard Trimble, Chris Van Wyk, Danica Woody, and Amy Young.

I am also grateful to home owners who permitted us behind otherwise closed doors, where we could enjoy their gracious interiors, beautiful outdoor settings, and magnificent

Acknowledgments

This marble fountain once graced a public square in Italy. Today it is the pride of an American powder room. The European fittings are nickel. A collection of hand towels adds a sophisticated touch.

views, including Sandra Erwin, Charles Faudree, Kristen Hebert, Muriel and Victor Hebert, Judy and Woodson Hobbs, Sara and Bradley Howell, Patricia and Jay McDonough, Tandy and Lee Roy Mitchell, Shelly and James Musselman, Christina and Bryce Phillips, Marilyn and Bruce Phillips, Nancy and Richard Robichaux, Kate Strasberg, Danica and Mark Woody, Chris and Wyn Van Wyk, and more.

A special thank you to Tara Archer, Judy Blackman, Bruno de la Croix-Vaubois, Barbara England, Rela Gleason, Harold Hand, Ellen Holt, Scott Jacques, Bill Mackin, Christie McRae, Joetta Moulden, George Nash, Kathleen Neeley, Alexandra Roach, Mary Jane Ryburn, Jayne Taylor, Gay Town, A. Hays Town, and Mike Williams.

Provençal Interiors: French Country Style in America is also the result of the hard work of editor Gail Yngve and book designer Traci O'Very Covey, whose creativity and talents helped shape this book.

Finally, a big thank you to my husband, John Roach, and our family for being supportive of this endeavor. Without their cooperation, this project would not be.

✤

Betty Lou Phillips

Wouldn't it be wonderful simply to close one's eyes,

make a wish, and unlock the door to a charming

French home, a home that reflects tastes, interests,

and lifestyle? It could be a place where the family

Introduction

traditions that bind us can grow and where memories

last forever or a place that is comfortable without

being complex and functional without being fussy. Put

another way, it would be grand to own a haven of

serenity that echoes the ambiance of France and cap-

tures the style of its people. ❖ The problem is seek-

ing a tidy definition of that fabled French style. In

France, the architecture, cuisine, and customs vary

from region to region, and at times even within regions.

So, not surprisingly, each of France's many provinces

has a unique character and charm. For centuries, the

This stately Louis XV stucco home reflects the ambiance and allure of old-world France, while providing state-of-the-art amenities for today's American lifestyle. Richly embellishing the exterior are quoin stones, a soaring slate roof, and cast-stone balustrades. Gracing the ends of rainspouts is the fleur-de-lis, the heraldic symbol of unity and harmony in France.

country's diverse climate and terrain hampered local traditions from being shared by the people nearby. Today, it is the blurring together of these ancient regional characteristics that has given life to the style known as provençal, or French country.

French country is the picture of understated luxury. Inspired by the sun-drenched colors of southern France, it is as fitting in the city and suburbs as in rural reaches, no matter that its modest roots are firmly planted in the small stone farmhouse, or *mas*—the typical dwelling in the region known as Provence. It is equally as appropriate in a remote château as in a stately manor house, called a *bastide*. The most inviting homes exude comfort, tradition, and grace. Many people, though, say it is *charm* that best characterizes the French interior.

At its finest, French country is the harmonious mingling of fabrics with soothing textures and pleasing patterns. It is the artistic blending of the reassuring feel of the familiar with warmth and sophistication—spaces flow, layouts function. Comfortably proportioned sofas and chairs invite family and friends to settle in. Also, a passion for finishing touches abounds.

In rooms staged with potted plants and cut flowers, family photographs claim prized spots. So do large handsomely carved armoires and other cherished pieces, passed down from generous aunts, uncles, and grandparents. Tracts of honey-colored sisal, chunky sea grass, and rugs from old châteaux relax on stone, tile, and hardwood floors. Impeccably tailored draperies boast piping, tassels, tiebacks, and fringes or lace curtains discreetly veil windows. Trims add personality to lamp shades and dressmaker touches to throw pillows. Unassuming collections evoke a look of old-world elegance.

Walls are painted, papered, upholstered, and sometimes cleverly feature trompe l'oeil—an optical illusion designed to delight the heart—which makes a flat surface appear three-dimensional. In French, *trompe* means to deceive or to trick; *l'oeil*, the eye. Fabric billows everywhere. It embraces tables, stretches across walls and inside wood pieces, tumbles from windows, and puddles on floors. In addition, it gracefully falls from canopy beds.

Beyond this, there is a mindfulness of four key elements—color, light, texture, and scale—which all flow from heightened awareness and a discriminating eye. Woven together, they affect the way it feels to be in a room.

Humble or grand, the architectural style of a house is less important than its furnishings and the way those furnishings mirror the life within. As a result, there is no "right" way to decorate. The French mix hand-me-downs with sought-after

This child-size chair covered in a tapestry may once have graced a Parisian living room, but today it stands proudly in an elegant San Francisco home. The worn fabric simply adds to its charm while the linen rug, woven in France, adds a touch of grandeur.

A French-country manor reminiscent of eighteenth-century France was designed for relaxed living. Interior spaces brim with deep fireplaces, timbered ceilings, weathered walls, and hardwoods. French doors open to a quiet backyard.

treasures found at flea markets or in their travels. Interiors are unpredictable and highly individual. For them, it would be unpardonable to live in a house full of new furniture with no reference to the past or any sentiment attached.

So how does one achieve the feeling of relaxed elegance in dwellings far from France? By starting to take a look at how designers on this side of the Atlantic capture the magic. Transcending national borders and time zones, French country takes many tantalizing turns when interpreted with American vision and verve.

As Americans fuse the spirit of America with the sophistication of France, they pay homage to a people who have, by example, taught them about glamour, style, and unerring taste. Fittingly, American

designers now share this know-how, reveal their secrets, and unabashedly demonstrate how to produce satisfying rooms with the feeling of well-being.

Indeed, the alluring spaces photographed for this book have a strong sense of beauty. But more importantly, they are interiors in which their occupants welcome friends, raise families, and celebrate meaningful occasions. These environments are infused with the vastly different personalities of the people who use them. There is no compromising their tastes or needs. Simply put, these spaces meet the criteria of well-designed rooms.

From fabrics and paint colors to furnishings and accessories, sumptuous rooms highlight elements essential to Provençal living. By demystifying design, interpreting good taste, and presenting an abundance of fresh options, solutions, and inspirations, American designers aim to raise consciousness and build confidence in the most apprehensive or novice decorator.

To be sure, it takes assurance to create warm gracious rooms intended for daily use—and a sharp eye for detail to develop them with true French panache. Still, with a design team of professionals leading the way, it's difficult to go wrong.

Of course, those who still have doubts about thinking things through by themselves can always turn to an interior designer for help. A designer can readily provide layout suggestions, color tips, and an overall plan. Sometimes all that is needed is a little direction, then a person is fine alone.

Naturally, planning and prioritizing are paramount in making a space work for individual styles of living. This is not to say decorating can't be fun or that it needs to be expensive—far from it. Eclectic furnishings from different eras peaceably mix, giving spaces a welcoming, less-serious air. If the wiring, heating, and plumbing in a home are in good shape, the things likely to be most expensive are fabric, painting, and perhaps some objects of affection, too.

Even if a newly found penchant for things French results in changing tastes and new attitudes, chances are one can use what he or she already owns, allowing a new mirror, rug, and collectibles to alter a room's character. Often, importing just one or two strong elements can create a country flavor, but then so can accessorizing with a lavish hand.

Whether a person wants to rethink one room or refresh an entire home, there is no need to toss everything out just to update. Still, it helps to take an objective look at how a space can better work with available furnishings by editing down to necessities and objects that have special meaning, then physically rebuilding from there. Once one figures out which pieces fit into the plans, moving furniture in, out, or about to achieve the desired look becomes easy.

A hearty admiration for all things French can be expressed readily with some paint, fresh drawer pulls, and a little ingenuity, giving old possessions new identity. Almost any chest or desk can acquire a country look when garnished with collectibles reminiscent of France—found at muddy flea markets, in family attics, and in antique shops.

Clearly, French country is about preserving slivers of the past, but better yet, it upholds today's design freedom. It is an expression of individuality as distinctive as one's personality, signature, and point of view. Paired with family heirlooms and salvage-yard finds that other people may never think of putting together, a room becomes a personal statement that is strictly one's own.

The wonders of a look, which is more than a style but also an attitude and a way of life, can be unlocked by roaming freely through this book. Imitation is indeed flattering. Still, the hope is that the ideas will become a source of motivation rather than models to copy, allowing one to bask in the satisfaction that comes from knowing the home is unmistakably his or her own, with its undeniable style and boundless charm.

After all, when it comes to decorating, a house should be a mirror of the people who live there, an environmental extension of who they are, patterned after the way they live. In any case, what should be reflected is the owner—re-creating the past, looking hopefully toward the future, and living presently in a home that is a wish fulfilled.

Trompe l'oeil wooden casks professedly filled with young wines supply an appropriate backdrop for this distinctive tasting room. The French limestone fireplace and groin-vaulted ceiling help create an intimate space for entertaining. A resplendent Persian Malayer carpet nearly 100 years old dresses up eighteenth-century terra-cotta transported from a European carriage house.

For some, charm is rich colors, a savvy mix of fabrics and patterns, and mellow old woods with warm patinas. For others, it is the luxury of comfort, interesting collections, and timeless elegance. And for still others,

WHAT IS *Provençal* CHARM?

Discreet details have a way of heightening awareness, inspiring one to focus more closely on the many touches that give rise to gracious living. Whether it is the carefully chosen pearl trim for a lamp shade, a collection of sterling frames filled with family photos, a table skirt caught with rosettes, or worry beads from one's travels—each makes a room more interesting and helps create a memorable setting. The table skirt material is from the French fabric house of Manuel Canovas.

it is the enchanting beauty found in details. No matter how it's defined, charm brings interiors to life, turning tastes and treasures into living works of art. When infused with a bit of smile-producing humor, it converts even the most serious settings into rooms where reality and creativity embrace. ⚜ Mostly, though, charm is personal. It is whatever one likes, whatever makes one feel good. Charm leaves lots of freedom for individual interpretation. Because it flows from the imagination, which knows no bounds, it is recognized as one sees it. Yet, its mystique lies in the intermingling of color, light, texture, and scale. All affect the spirit of a room. Beyond how a room looks, it is important how it feels.

✤   C O L O R   ✤

Color is a powerful element in design. Used wisely, it can raise ceilings, lengthen walls, highlight architectural details, and diminish flaws. Also, researchers say that it can influence moods, arouse senses, or soothe souls.

With color the character of a room can be changed from prim to cozy or from peaceful to upbeat. Cool colors—greens, blues, and purples—have a restful effect, while warm colors—reds, oranges, browns, and yellows—create a stimulating, cheerful atmosphere. Vibrant pigments can transform a room from dull to dramatic or promise a bright look on a bleak day.

Color also can make spaces appear larger or smaller than they are. Rich, deep colors make rooms feel snug and intimate by seemingly shrinking settings. Softer, lighter colors foster a sense of space. But even the same color combinations used in varying proportions can alter a room's dynamics by giving it a slightly different spin. One of the secrets behind the French look is the artful use of color.

In any scheme, hues that share the same value or amount of lightness or darkness generally create a harmonious feeling. Also capable of delighting the eye are tints of a single base color, which are produced by adding varying amounts of white to colors that are too dark. For example, both pink and rose are tints of red. Slowly adding black to a base color that lacks depth creates a shade. Berry first, then wine results when black is added to red. We can produce thousands of shades and

tints by adding black or white. Intensity is the saturation, or degree of purity, of a color. For example, fern, moss, cypress, and hunter are all greens; however, they differ in strength.

Many Americans prefer monochromatic rooms—rooms built around one color. The French instinctively long for settings with the very elements that attract so many summer visitors to Provence—rich vibrant colors, subdued earth tones, magical light. Drawing from the radiance of nature, French interiors are a kaleidoscope celebrating the land, sun, and sea.

Breathtaking blues appear in a spectrum of tints and shades, ranging from the cobalt blue that gracefully rises from the Mediterranean, to the pale blue of the sky, to the violet blue of lavender beds. Snipped from blooms in nearby flower gardens, rooms revel in brilliant sunflower

The seductive back of this elegantly shaped sofa quickly catches the eye, beckoning one into an interior that is warm and inviting. The Versailles sofa is a work of art from the Cameron Collection at George Cameron Nash, Dallas, while the Harlequin quilted silk is from Nancy Corzine in Los Angeles.

yellow and glorious poppy red, deep scarlet and rich terra-cotta. But brights are not the only colors at home. The leafy greens and the stony grays of the rolling French countryside work, too. Color also takes a cue from the olives, plums, and vineyard grapes in revelry to the earth that produced them. Finally, in a country entrenched in its fabled past, old-world shades of ochre, sienna, and umber are among those fancied.

*A*mericans may be people who wield influence around the globe, but when it comes to the color wheel, our powers of persuasion fail to gain it greater acceptance among the French. "We have no rules about anything," Duc de Choiseul, the eccentric court minister of Louis XV, pithily pointed out centuries ago. "Rules are like shackles; pleasure cannot abide them," he added, summing up the French attitude. Perhaps not, but while the French forsake the color wheel, Americans remain keenly aware of its usefulness.

Fabrics, furniture, floor coverings, and flowers vie with one another for the pleasure of introducing color to a room. So does everything from tiles, paints, wall coverings, and works of art to accessories. Yet, not everyone feels confident when working with color. In fact, many people are intimidated by it. For them, planning a palette, which is the range of colors within a composition, from the dizzying array of options can be a daunting task. No matter that it is color that elevates their spirits or that they are bored with beige. They take refuge in the unassuming neutrals rather than trusting any more adventuresome instincts or taking advantage of the power of paint.

Still, there is no need to plan around risk-free white if the warmth of color makes a person happier. The trickiest part about working with color is identifying the hues one likes, which really isn't all that difficult to do. Using personal preferences as a starting point, it's easy to come up with the colors one prefers. Whether one is a color connoisseur or not, the closet is a valid place to look when seeking inspirations for a room. It can offer clues to the colors one finds comforting.

When planning a palette, a favorite element can serve as the springboard for layering color and other elements in a room. Some designers begin by anchoring a setting with a splendid carpet, and letting it suggest the room's colors. Others routinely plan around an inviting patterned fabric. A painted chest, a collection, or a work of art also are ideal beginnings. Moreover, any piece with an irresistible draw will work.

Although one can certainly use as wide a palette as desired, designers generally opt for three colors, and no more than four, to unite the sundry elements in a

In an interior awash with color and texture, a pleasing mix of French and English influences bridges the gap between two cultures. An oil of Countess Montalban of Montpellier adds a dramatic bit of glamour. It was painted in 1842 by Joseph-Désiré Court, whose work appears in the Louvre. The piano is also an object of beauty.

room. Visually, too many colors can be overwhelming to the eye. With a bevy of excitement, it bounces around searching for a resting spot, which not only can be unsettling but can also prove difficult to live with over time.

However, it is not necessary for the same three colors to weave throughout a house, cottage, or high-rise. Each room needs a spirit of its own. The personality of the living room, for example, should be as distinct from an adjoining garden room as the garden room is from the library. It is much more interesting to look through a doorway into a neighboring room where the color scheme varies.

Seeing room after room of color copies is boring. Yet the truth is, a house *does* work best if one space flows into another, and, it is *infinitely* more pleasing when the dominant color in an adjoining area is complementary to the adjacent area, visually linking the rooms from setting to setting.

Plainly, small rooms give the illusion of appearing larger when fewer colors are used. For this reason, some designers settle on diluted shades of one color, encouraging the eye to sweep across close quarters. Others prefer the more dramatic use of intense colors and bold patterns. Clearly, not everyone agrees on what's best. The French insist nothing creates the feeling of spaciousness more than uninterruptedly swathing a room in bolts of a single understated print. In keeping with this philosophy, Francophiles—and others—have been unifying settings by lavishly repeating the same fabric on windows, walls, and upholstery since the early eighteenth century, before wallpaper was popular. Even today, Europeans-of-means still use fabric for lining walls more often than Americans.

There's no denying that the place-ment of color is as important as the palette and that balance is the foundation of a comfortable scheme. Most people feel uncomfortable if a room isn't balanced. Repeating major colors helps pull a room together. Using color effectively, however, can be challenging, even for a decorator. Taking cues from the rooms shown here will make creating a rhythm a little easier, but one shouldn't hesitate to use a designer as a consultant if necessary. Doing so may avoid making a costly mistake.

Some gifted artists determine areas of weakness in their paintings by turning them upside down. Interior designers use their mind's eye to balance settings and envision how compositions will actually look. Their strategy includes taking colors from rugs, wallcoverings, and fabrics, embedding them in their minds, then mentally toting them around the room while asking, Might this area be too busy, or Does that spot need something else? By juggling elements, not only do they stimulate their imaginations into planning details, but they also fuse disparate thoughts until finally their canvases become crafted and complete.

When coming up with a palette, the color wheel—a universal tool—is helpful in understanding the way hues relate to one another. However, it is best used simply as a guide since most colors used in design schemes are altered in ways that soften their impact. Besides, the French snub the color wheel, maintaining that society cannot improve on nature, whose colors never clash, translating into a nearly anything-goes attitude. Obviously, anyone can have fun experimenting with color combinations, or one can consider some seasoned favorites. At its simplified best, four time-honored plans emanate from wheel relationships.

✤ Monochromatic ✤

Monochromatic colors lend a sophisticated look that relies on assorted tints or shades of a single color, for example, parchment, café au lait, and caramel, which are all in the brown family. Tones that melt into one another create an airy soothing feeling, making rooms appear more spacious than they actually are by seducing the eye into roaming easily over walls, carpet, and upholstery without focusing on any one piece. When working with the subtle nuances of one color, juxtaposing both sumptuous and modest textures adds interest to a room and gives it character.

✤ Analogous ✤

Analogous, or neighboring colors that are adjacent to each other on the wheel, produce refreshing yet refined rooms. Some examples are blue and green, blue with a green cast, or blue with a purple cast, which is a hint rather than high contrast of another hue. Schemes can be created from any place on the wheel. Simply by picking a favorite color or a diluted shade or tint, one then looks to either side or just one side if preferred. The color next to it acts as an accent. Again, equal values of varying hues are appealing to the eye.

✤ Triadic ✤

Any three colors equidistant from each other are winning combinations. A room can be brightened with yellow, red, and blue, or a playful assortment of orange, purple, and green. Color-saturated hues have long been identified with Provençal style. Softening sun-kissed tones create a more mellowed look.

✤ Complementary ✤

Contrasting colors from opposite

Taking its cue from the garden room's hand-smocked, diamond-patterned curtain heading, this table skirt merits high praise. The picture frames amicably mix rather than match the Pierre Frey stripe, Clarence House check, and Brunschwig & Fils solid used in the room. The area rug is from Stark Carpet.

sides of the color wheel bring vitality to settings. Red and green are complements, so are blue and orange, and yellow and purple. When drenching rooms in two bold colors, it is helpful to liken them to a stage production in which one color is the star and the other mindfully stays in the background in a manner befitting the set. Otherwise, the two colors will compete shamelessly for eye-catching attention. Also, daring combinations such as strong

Many of the furnishings in this light-filled living room honor Louis XV, but amid the serene palette, there also is an eclectic mix of pieces from other eras and places such as the chaise shown. A vintage Fortuny fabric dresses up an eighteenth-century Venetian-style chair, gilded then given a color-washed finish. The oak flooring was cut on an angle before being set in a classical pattern, and hand scraped and hand scrubbed. French doors create a tie with the outside world.

green and clear red can always be toned down to pine and claret, which may be better suited to one's comfort level. Yellow and purple can become straw and lavender, much like Impressionist painter Claude Monet's haystacks.

✤ LIGHT ✤

Color is light, so how a person perceives color is dependent upon how waves of light reflected from nearby surfaces are discerned. Color is never stationary. The location of the sun or shadows from a passing cloud can alter the way a color appears. Sunlight contains rays of red, yellow, orange, green, blue, and violet. It reflects these hues in varying amounts, depending upon the surfaces it strikes.

Light plays off colors, furnishings, and textures differently. Some surfaces reflect light and some absorb it. Furniture finishes generate their own glow. Whether

Tips for Using Color

❧ Let the size of the room and the mood you want to create influence your choice of color. To give cramped quarters the feeling of space, use light cool colors on walls and ceilings. To make a large room less imposing, use dark warm colors. Actually, there's nothing wrong with painting any size room a dark color if it is a cozy look you are after. However, bold colors work best in large rooms with a lot of light, or in powder rooms and entries where you spend limited time.

❧ Walls with rich, saturated paint colors look best at night when rooms are artificially lit. In the daylight, deep colors highlight wall imperfections. Consider masking uneven walls, or ones with odd angles, with patterned wallcoverings.

❧ Paint a low ceiling a lighter color than the walls and moldings. You will draw the eye upward, thus creating the illusion of greater height. If you paint the walls, trim, and ceiling the same color, you will visually lift the ceiling even more. A ceiling color darker than the walls perceptually lowers the ceiling. Striped wallcovering can also make a low-slung ceiling look taller. Use a level to keep the stripes straight if hanging the paper yourself.

❧ When a house has distinguishing features, underscore them if they are significant. Architectural embellishments such as crown moldings, window casings, and baseboards deserve some attention. Set them apart by framing walls in a contrasting color.

❧ Accentuate strong colors, such as deep brown, with white trim. Muted colors such as moss green call for dark floors and subdued oyster trim, but white is easy to age. You can also add depth and character by choosing a trim color several shades deeper than the walls, then topping it with a decorative painting technique.

❧ To mask an architectural flaw, avoid highlighting it. Instead, reduce telltale signs by painting the feature the same color as the wall. This is easy to do when it is an unseemly radiator to which you object. But what about a fireplace that is in need of a facelift? Fortunately, there are a number of ways for dealing with it, too. By flanking it with two chairs covered in the same vibrant print, you will create a new focus.

❧ You can also add style to an unexciting mantelpiece by stripping and refinishing it. If there isn't a mantelpiece for your treasures, the solution may be as close as the nearest lumberyard. Still, keep in mind that any new additions should be in proportion to the scale of the room. Also, there are a number of places to buy a detailed fireplace surround; flea markets and back rooms of antiques stores are two likely spots to look.

❧ Trends come and go, so it is best to avoid faddish colors that soon look dated. Once you come up with a color you'd like to live with—from the flower garden or wherever—have it computer-matched at your local paint store. Some programs allow you to feed a photo of your room into the computer, then test the colors you are considering.

✤ There is no substitute, however, for trying a color in the space you are thinking about using it. Often the color on a paint card bears little resemblance to a wall color. Even when it does, it is useful to study a color at different times of the day in changing light before making any decisions. If possible, pick up some half-pint testers in the various colors you are considering and brush three-by-three-foot swatches on white poster boards, then tack them on the walls.

✤ If you are looking for a lengthening effect, vertical stripes can make even a scant hallway look longer. In rooms with low ceilings, they heighten the feeling. The width of the stripe is critical, however. For positive results, it should complement the size and shape of the room. Pinstripes in a large room will blur together, while large-scale stripes in a small room can overpower the space. Decorative painting techniques such as sponging, ragging, or stippling add interest. For a mottled look, a wet sponge is dipped in paint, then dabbed against the wall. In ragging, an artist's rag is patted over wet paint. Stippling results when the tip of a paintbrush creates tiny dots on a wet wall. Successful application of any decorative paint finish requires some research.

✤ Water-based latex paints are easiest to work with. They dry quickly, are nearly odorless, and clean up with soap and water. Paints come in three finishes: gloss, semigloss, and low gloss, which are also called flat, satin, or eggshell. Flat paint works tenaciously at hiding wall and ceiling imperfections. It also exudes the French look, where the most sought-after surface is a patina nearing years of use. For all its virtues, however, flat paint also has its faults. The duller the paint, the less it withstands washing and wear. This is why the more scrubbable semigloss and gloss paints are popular choices for trim, doors, and cabinets.

✤ There is no disputing that color can affect human behavior by stimulating certain emotions. For example, red can raise your blood pressure. But when fiery red is toned down to a more earthy red, it looses its brashness and is deeply comforting. A library resplendent in red then takes on a refined air, producing the perfect backdrop for books, wood pieces, and art—especially when partnered with textured fabrics in camel, tobacco, or timber brown. In a small entry, it is warmly welcoming. Transported to the dining room, sophisticated crimson red appeals to the palate, complements wood pieces, and sets an intimate mood for entertaining. In the candlelight company of creamy fabrics and linen trim, it casts a flattering glow. Pair it with glimmering gold for traditional richness, or layer it with various textures and values of red for lighthearted glamour.

✤ With its skylike clearness, restful blue is so comforting that it is seldom used in schools. In homes, it soothingly bestows the feeling of well-being. The experts say yellow is uplifting, but some colorists don't consider it an appropriate choice for bedrooms since it is known to speed up the metabolism. Because soft greens reduce nervous and muscular tension, they are often used in hospital rooms. The stronger greens, such as forest and hunter, are ideal for snug spaces with lots of books and rooms with a clubby or lodge look.

"A thing of beauty is a joy forever, its loveliness increases," wrote John Keats, the British poet. This elegant Louis XV walnut commode, circa 1760, is from the south of France. Its tired drawers are upholstered in Christopher Norman's Brittany silk plaid.

rough or smooth, brushed or burnished, each piece catches and holds light in its own way. However subtle, a balance between shadow and light is essential in creating a becoming setting.

Too much light is jarring and casts unforgiving shadows on the face as the French point out matter-of-factly. Predictably, skin tones and furnishings revel in flattering, softly lit spaces exuding a romantic mood. The French shun track lighting. Rather, diffused lighting is a key element in their homes. It emanates from the layering of candles, sconces, picture lights, and carefully placed table and floor lamps with low-wattage bulbs. Shimmering faceted and prism-cut chandeliers catch the light, multiplying it, bringing instant drama into rooms.

An ocean away, Americans join the French in capitalizing on the chandelier's reflective properties. Fixtures are hung so that images are cast back in mirrors whenever possible, which results in giving spaces depth. Here, dimmers adjust light levels downward from bright to the kindest glow, creating an aura of peaceful well-being. For reading, Americans prefer high-wattage frosted bulbs and three-way switches. Another American preference is to arrange lamps in a triangle rather than placing them in four corners where they cast isolated islands of light, knowing, of course, that lamp shades, fabrics, and floor coverings have an impact on the way color catches the light.

Before selecting colors and furnishings, most American designers study the natural light in a room because it influences what will look best. Warm colors work well in settings with northern exposures, making hues appear cooler. Cool colors soak up excess warmth and sunshine in rooms with southern light.

✤   T E X T U R E   ✤

The French are masters at layering pattern and textures in endless subtle ways that make interiors both blissfully comfortable and supremely sensuous. The key is in the magical way they pull things together—the furniture, the accessories, the lush palettes of France. At first glance, settings appear uncomplicated until one studies how they are composed.

Starting with roughly troweled walls, a *glaze* coat, or a finishing technique, adds depth, imparting a softer, richer surface that reflects light differently than paint. Next, a pleasant mix of fabric weaves transforms flat planes into areas more three-dimensional. Finally, there is a dramatic interplay of contrasts that complement each other—strong with soft, light with dark, old with new, sophisticated with relaxed, sumptuous with humble, and rigid with fluid. Meters of fabrics—some luxurious, others their more common cousins—deftly team with slate, iron, woven rush, and other natural materials, achieving balance and creating settings that are highly liveable, charming, and hospitable.

Curiously enough, a room with few textures produces the feeling of space, but an intriguing mix of textures and shapes—on walls, furnishings, and floors—is considerably more interesting. To keep shapes from competing with one another, it's best to avoid placing two objects the same size or shape side by side. Rather, nestling round forms amidst rectangular, square, and oval ones is more eye-pleasing. This isn't to say strong shapes should not be repeated within a room, creating a sense of unity. It is only to suggest that they are varied, too. Similarly, since two wood pieces are less than neighborly, one can offset their hard surfaces by lavishing fabric nearby.

Unquestionably, smooth textures communicate a more refined spirit than rough textures, which are more casual. This is a result of smooth surfaces catching the light, exuding a sheen or warmer finish. Warmest of all is the unmistakable patina of old wood enriched by age. Fabrics that gleam—silks, taffetas, and moirés—convey a dressier feeling than textured fabrics such as denims and other wovens, which cast shadows. Shadows mask the light, veiling colors or making them appear darker and duller than they are.

✤   S C A L E   ✤

Consciously or not, the distinctive scale of furnishings is the first thing one notices upon entering a French home. The reason is simple. History reminds us that for centuries the French have favored large-scale furniture and accessories that are refined but generously proportioned.

Although large houses throughout France have, with time, given way to less-spacious ones with smaller rooms, furnishings still have the oversized look expected when the custom of handing down family heirlooms remains unchanged, never mind that these legacies might be somewhat overwhelming for their less-roomy new settings. Rooms are defined around them. Far more meaningful are the ancestral ties that bring pieces of the past to present-day spaces.

Besides, generously sized pieces compatibly pick up on the large-scale proportions that typify French rooms, and since this is the scale the eye is accustomed to seeing, it is maneuvered into enlarging its perception of an area. Spaces are filled with only inches to spare, and somehow, even the smallest living quarters become grander.

Appropriately then, interiors merit furnishings that are imposing. Integrating boldly scaled, dignified old wood pieces can be challenging, however. Unless the right pieces find their way to the right places, their attention-grabbing presence can alarmingly slant the visual weight to one side of a room. But being French means a certain predisposition for an innate sense of proportion and a discerning eye. Balance, not symmetry, is generally the secret behind successful settings.

Fittingly, rooms are dressed in majestic armoires with dramatically curved bonnets, commodes with intriguing hardware, and splendid desks and console tables whose gracefully carved cabriole legs back up to roomy sofas. Desks and consoles are at least 60 inches long and, more commonly, impressively longer. The best scale for those backing up to 84- to 101-inch sofas requires leaving no more than 12 inches of sofa exposed on a side.

Stately hutches, or *vaisseliers,* and buffets—one in two pieces is called a *buffet à deux corps,* and one that has a series of doors is called an *enfilade*—clearly add stature. But these are not just aesthetic choices. More often they are practical answers satisfying the need for storage and serving space in rooms. In tribute to their fabled sense of style, however, passionate Francophiles think nothing of serving from buffets 40 to 42 inches tall. To their way of thinking, pieces this height are more attractive than lower ones, so ease is not a priority.

Cushy, overscaled sofas—with sumptuous rolled arms—are pleasantly plump but not so feather-stuffed that occupants feel unimportant. Instead, both sofas and chairs simply invite one to sink into their ample proportions and stay put in the comfort of big downy pillows that, even from a distance, add drama.

More than anything, charm evolves from a collection of liberally scaled garnishes that elevate the ordinary. The trims embellishing throw pillows are full rather than skimpy, which can often be attributed to the fact that they are doubled. The costly *bullions,* or thick twisted fringes that give upholstery a more sophisticated look, are deep rather than shallow. Quiet old wood pieces no longer stand shyly in the background when painted then embellished with lush ribbon-wrapped bouquets, graceful garlands, and faux marble tops. Sweeping curtains, luxuriously constructed with hidden interlining, speak for themselves while mingling easily with finely crafted finials and rods.

Whereas small paintings would disappear on generous walls when grouped together with wall sconces and mirrors, they make a strong statement. Large, admirably framed mirrors create the illusion of depth. Meanwhile, heroic-sized family portraits invariably add splendor and historic character.

Dismissing the American practice of leaving 8 to 18 inches of exposed wood around the perimeter of a room, ample-sized area rugs travel across once-forbidden

One might guess this is a generously sized living room; however, it is anything but that. An intimate room benefits from a strong focal point, supported by distinctive ample-sized pieces. Here, a sophisticated Summer Hill print with an extravagant thirty-six-inch horizontal repeat adorns the sofa. Tightly arranged botanicals in similar frames help make an even stronger statement. Definitely capable of standing alone is an antique cupboard. A boldly scaled Brunschwig & Fils chenille plaid covers the bergère chairs.

lines, making rooms appear bigger than they are and smaller carpets look skimpy.

Even in small rooms, the French think big, opting for a few furnishings, always exaggerated in size rather than more modestly scaled, mainly because scaled-up pieces convincingly suggest roominess. But more than a feeling of spaciousness is nourished by a sparsely furnished arrangement. Individual pieces are more readily appreciated when there is room to notice their features. Creating breathing space and circulating room around spotlighted sofas and chairs makes entertaining more enjoyable, too.

Although many people mistakenly think that small unassuming furnishings work best in tight places, this simply isn't true. Most intimate spaces profit from the commanding look of a few large pieces that help mask a room's smallness and keep it from feeling cluttered. In contrast, crowding limited space with more moderately scaled furnishings can make a small room seem even smaller.

There is no denying that design is as much about what is left out of a space as what is put in it. The old Mies van der Rohe adage, *less is more*, applies soundly to the process.

The garden room came of age during the twentieth century in densely populated Paris, London, Rome, and New York. Spurred by the glass houses constructed by Europe's nobility, home owners began enclosing their terraces and improving gloomy corridors by installing large windows and potted palms. The garden room's beginnings, however, may date back to 1686 when the Orangerie at Versailles was built to house Louis XIV's citrus trees, though some say protective houses for plants came into existence centuries earlier.

The garden beyond, filled with beautiful urns and fragrant boughs, offered endless inspiration for scheming this conservatory. The wood trim and matchstick blinds borrow nature's celadon green. Terra-cotta walls take their cue from the tiled rooftop. In a style of their own, stencil motifs echo vines scaling the side of the house.

The weathered walls, sisal rug, chenille throw, and hand-painted silk pillows, inspired by the Travers botanical on the love seats, easily arouse the senses. Wood trim draws additional interest to lined and interlined shades. An old dish drainer serves as a planter while resting upon a cast-stone-and-iron table. Nearby, the Louis XV pine buffet-à-deux corps, circa 1840, houses a collection of vintage silver, originally used in the grand hôtels, restaurants, and cafés of Europe.

A soul drenched in art history reveres good bones—architectural features original to the room, such as a high ceiling, paneled doors, and parquet flooring. When they do not exist, some designers delight in giving bland spaces architectural character. Here, the living area streams into the entry, and the entry drifts into the dining room, generating the feeling of oneness, but it was not always so. Fine craftsmanship and artfully layered color transformed these once-ordinary spaces into those that now have the look of an eighteenth-century petite château.

This triadic scheme emanates from the boisterous play of yellows, reds, and blues. White trim casually defines the setting, but Provençal red is the palette's center. The faux-finished coffee table serves as the focal point, while yellow and blue quietly balance the room, making it comfortable for year-round use.

This library is wrapped in the unexpected combination of caramel, black, and opera red, while demonstrating that scaled-up furnishings such as the antique Louis XV desk and French-made leopard-print wool rug work well in small rooms. Portraits of family members are suspended from brass chains tacked to picture rails—grooved molding mounted just below the ceiling—to avoid damaging the glazed walls. Shelves spill over with books. Across the way, a standing lamp sides a generous sofa, creating an inviting reading spot.

Fastidiously placed lighting paired with oversized furnishings, thick chenilles, and soft fabrics with large repeats warm a meandering space with lofty proportions. Sculpture, art, and antiques add character.

No matter that this buffet once had more than its share of nicks and scratches. Seeing its potential, the designer picked it up inexpensively, then transformed it with coats of paint. Glazing elevated its character. However, by putting it in a place of honor, he gave it even more esteem.

Subtle glazing adds a French flavor to the hand-stenciled ribbons and bows on walls, suggesting age. Glazing also takes the dining table in a newly refined direction, setting it apart from other reproductions. Unassuming plants, overflowing from magnificent urns, rim the setting, confirming that they are as appropriate in the dining room as they are on the terrace. Walnut flooring, installed in a herringbone pattern, adds to the interior's enchantment.

The entrance hall is not merely a thoroughfare for approaching more important rooms, nor is it an area solely for welcoming guests. Although not necessarily a room, it has the power to wordlessly set the am-

Making AN ENTRANCE

biance of a house and serve as an important introduction to the interior. ❧ It is not by chance, then, that French homes have a way of making a positive first impression. Great efforts go into transforming this potentially serviceable space into an unapologetically elegant setting, which encourages curiosity and exudes an air of intimacy. ❧ French standards call for architectural details in the entrance hall to be as gracefully rendered as in any major room. In towering châteaux, thick soaring stone walls are carved into

A sweeping staircase wrapped in black and drizzled with gold brings drama to a foyer with French limestone floors. The Louis XV walnut commode contributes a touch of eighteenth-century elegance while the baby-grand piano tucked into the curve pleasurably plays to a generous room. Walls hung with deckle-edged, stipple-patterned blocks simulating limestone, further the welcoming atmosphere.

stately archways and buttresses, defining passageways between rooms. Intricate ornamental ironwork wraps grand curving staircases as might be expected since the French have long been renowned for their skill in making magnificent objects from iron.

Hand-finished plaster walls are a fitting backdrop for sophisticated but unassuming furniture in other homes with lofty proportions. Landing windows, framed with rich Louis XV molding, bathe the house in light. Wood plank doors add an even stronger architectural presence, particularly when finished with a wash and finely crafted hardware. In early French houses, floors were often stone or native tile. Today, they also are laid with hardwoods, limestone, and marble.

Handsome timbered ceilings emit an air of nonchalance in rural dwellings where steep narrow stairwells spiral to spare rooms. Since clay is plentiful in pastoral French provinces, many homes still have unglazed terra-cotta tile floors, which are easy to keep up in the constant battle against dirt. Runners fend off the chill of cold floors and stifle noise.

Textured, glazed walls exude an aged worn look that is a much different look from a painted wall. For centuries, glazing has been practiced by artists, who discovered it was one of the many ways to modify color and disguise wall defects. Washed in a coat of translucent color that signals classic French style, the painted surface is toned down, producing varying results depending on the base and top coats used. For example, sand over milky white achieves the appearance of worn parchment. Amber over butterscotch creates a warm mellowing terra-cotta.

Whether it is decorative painting, a tile floor, or fine cabinetry, the French

seek quality old-world craftsmanship to enhance the beauty of their homes. To them, professional-looking results mean turning these projects over to experts with well-honed skills. What they expect in return is a level of workmanship that, more often than not, only money can buy. Like most people we know, the French splurge on things that are important to them and economize on others, but they are famous for their stubborn insistence on quality.

Although they are not believers in the showy or the contrived, the French look upon even the smallest entry as an ever-expanding art gallery, thinking vertically in soaring spaces. Rather than stuffing the space with furniture, a congenial mix of paintings, drawings, prints, and photographs jostle for wall space with even more paintings, drawings, prints, and

An eighteenth-century radassié, or banquette, that seats three has all the French hallmarks—hand carving, a double-woven rush seat, and a plush cushion. The hand-painted pillows are silk. Paintings lining the hall are eclectically framed.

A suitably grand door with magnificent decorative ironwork opens to a sprawling entrance, where close friends are warmly welcomed with kisses on both cheeks in keeping with the traditional European practice. Stone-colored tiles draw attention to an exquisite floor. A round table is a becoming centerpiece with a towering arrangement of the season's best blooms.

photographs hung above and below. Fresh flowers, scented candles, and sleepy dogs that have been in the family for years also greet guests. An array of big ceramic pots hold umbrellas and dog leashes.

To be sure, the French favor objets d'art—small art objects—that bring elegance and a touch of history to settings. But they equate elegance with restraint. So it is the charm of everyday things— porcelain plates, wooden boxes, decanters, antique canes, a shawl or a quilt draped over a table—that make their entrances special. Not only do they lounge in places other than originally intended, they have meticulous attention bestowed upon them.

Assembling and arranging objets d'art—in a seemingly *effortless* way—is a trait at which the French excel. Spaces do not look overly thought out. Rather, accessories appear to have offhandedly found their own way to spots. Few, however, realize that nothing is ever left to chance. Only those who know how particular the French are, are aware it could be otherwise, and, indeed, this is what makes settings so charming!

❧ FRENCH CONNECTIONS ❧

Unquestionably, a hall or foyer is not where one spends a lot of time, so it can be hard to think imaginatively about improving it. Still, plants, paint, and a little planning can transform even the plainest entry into an endearing setting, tailored to its potential. Truth be told, rousing a French-country mood can be as effortless as inviting Mother Nature inside the front door.

For ages, the French have been filling their entries with vines, berries, and seed pods. Armfuls of freshly gathered branches are also worked into arrangements. An old wire plant stand nestled against the wall can look captivating stuffed with seasonal plants, including small trailing ivies that spill gracefully into the room.

Lush healthy plants in large terracotta or ceramic pots can also brighten a foyer. One should cover the soil with moss and sprinkle a bit in the saucers, letting available sunlight guide in the choice of plants. Of course, it is easy to find plants for well-lit spots near east, west, or southern exposures. Low-light sites pose more of a challenge, but many plants will flourish in these areas, too: among them— bird's-nest ferns, Chinese evergreens, dieffenbachia, heart-leaf philodendrons, Janet Craig dracaenas, kentia palms, grape ivies, and spathiphyllum. Though a person may feel obliged to add leaf-shining to the list of monthly tasks, plants growing in low light won't need watering or feeding as often as those growing in well-lit spots.

If space permits, a ladderback, rush-bottom *banquette* can quickly give a French flavor, especially when an unexpected combination of overscale plaids and flowering pillows rest upon it. Underfoot, tile, stone, or brick flooring heighten a welcoming feeling. Hardwood floors stained the same color can link a series of rooms together, while wide hardwoods left bare can make a narrow entrance appear larger.

Some Americans, with a passion for books that surpasses shelf space, are turning their entryways into auxiliary libraries by building floor-to-ceiling bookcases around doorways and along walls. If one's foyer simply isn't roomy enough, one could consider stacking a few hardcover garden, architecture, or art books on a skirted round table, where they can double as bases for prized collectibles. A *tablescape,* or grouping of objects on a tabletop, looks best if there's an amiable mix of tall, medium, and small—softened by a single flower in a vase.

Dress up an inexpensive plywood

This thoughtfully appointed entry stacked high with art and antiques ushers visitors into a home with pleasing symmetry. The ensemble, gathered in and around Paris, includes the French national flag. The republican Tricolore replaced the fleur-de-lis as the symbol of France after the revolution in 1789.

table with a pretty floor-length skirt. A hidden inner lining will give it body, pushing it away from the table in a disciplined way. An unlined tableskirt can attract unwanted attention, while a skimpy table can look out of proportion. The best results come from a thirty-inch-tall table that is at least thirty inches in diameter, while thirty-six inches is even better. Since design is always the sum of well-planned vignettes, let a lamp—mounted on books for height—prove the point. It is easy to give a plain shade some cache by embellishing with braid or narrow ribbons, using fabric glue.

Another workable plan starts with a narrow console table, or a pretty commode, or chest, where guests can place their handbags. Whether the piece is old or a good reproduction, scale is key. For a country look, it should nearly fill the wall. Over a chest, it is attractive to center a mirror that is narrower by four to six inches on each side. Above all, the two pieces should not match. Capturing the spontaneity of the French is easiest if the pieces merely work together rather than appearing store-bought with matching woods and finishes.

In an entrance with a high ceiling, a chandelier and a grandfather's clock can add warmth, but one shouldn't be deterred by an eight-foot ceiling in need of architectural help. Adding inexpensive stock molding around windows, baseboards, and where the ceiling meets the walls can trick the eye into perceiving greater height. Extending the crown molding onto the ceiling makes a space appear even taller by reducing the ceiling area that is exposed. A good rule of thumb for determining what size molding to use is— the taller the ceiling, the more profuse the molding, and vice versa.

One need not stop by simply adding moldings in rooms that lack it. Textured walls exude a graciousness that smooth walls cannot. Alternatively, wallcovering may be worth considering. A wide tone-on-tone stripe can coax the eye upward, seemingly heightening a space. In areas with no distinguishing architectural elements, a trompe l'oeil border can inexpensively create a finished look.

However, there should never be a clue as to what is old and what is new. Walls, flooring, and furnishings with a proud past should all work together warmly, welcoming visitors. Without the feeling of a bygone age, there is a chance that any room will look designed, and, as might be expected, the best spaces never look decorated.

Hand-painted sisal carpets this back stairway while hand-painted ivy clambers up the stucco walls.

There's no reason a back entrance should not look stylish, too, since it is through here that the family generally detours when going in and out. Outfitting this ordinary back way—in an eighteenth-century way—is a collection of botanical cutouts glued directly to powder room and laundry doors.

In France, the living room envelops the family's most cherished furniture and objets d'art. An inherited armoire almost inevitably dominates the room, one

French QUARTERS

with deep carving and the patina that comes only with age is the quintessential French-country piece. Indeed, the French have an appreciation for vintage pieces with sentimental value, not a price tag. Even an armoire that is far from a showpiece can lend a bit of grandeur with a story from its past, which is another way of saying the armoire is not disturbing if it boldly upstages other elements in the room. ⚜ Likewise, it does not matter that guests must choose from a potpourri of mismatched chairs—all of which can be

Naples yellow was one of Napoleon's favorite colors—along with Prussian blue, which projected the prestige of his rule. He was also fond of stripes and used them lavishly in decorating both his state and private homes. The burnished Louis XVI ribbon salon chairs wear the same delicate Scalamandré yellow, coffee, and cream silk as the window treatment. The linen rug was loomed in France.

easily moved where needed in the eighteenth-century manner. Each has been chosen for its proportion, balance, and graceful lines rather than its royal lineage. For the French, the feeling of harmony is more important than sameness. Long ago, furniture was lined stiffly around the perimeter of a room. Today, chairs are congenially grouped to promote both warm intimate conversations and lively discussions. The French have a thoughtful gracious approach to entertaining, which requires seating for the same number of people in the salon as in the dining room, allowing discussions to continue following dinner and dessert.

Though the French believe in living in aesthetically created spaces, overly serious rooms do not make sense in many modern homes, nor do rarely used untouchable places defined by velvet ropes. Their life is fueled by a love for family, a devotion to pets, and an affection for one's country. Even in rooms rich with Aubusson pillows and rare antiques, children's books and toys are scattered amid the collectibles, and though there may be impressive artwork, rooms exude a friendly aura suited to family life.

The message gleaned is that furniture is intended to be used but not abused, which is not a problem. For French children, good manners are a must. Additionally, from an early age their eyes are honed with keen appreciation for good furniture and fine antiques. Remarkably, by their teens many have absorbed the *bon goût*, or exquisite taste, of their quality-conscious parents. An interest in the arts is both nurtured and encouraged by parents who shepherd their young to museums as often as they shepherd them to playgrounds.

While children are taught to love and respect finery, family dogs are pampered,

leading enviable lives. When *le chien* is not getting fluffed and manicured, it is aptly an accessory, setting off madame's serious jewelry—without being too obvious about it, of course. Practically speaking, this means the smaller the dog the better. From dawn until well past nightfall, amiable animals known by their personality, not their pedigree, are toted everywhere—through the arches of old Métro stations, into nearby bistros, to the movies, and even to the most chic restaurants where menus feature special meals for well-mannered pets.

❧ FURNISHINGS ❧

With the country's ten million dogs, or one for every five citizens—playing a major role in family life, having the run of houses, and lolling happily on the furniture—practicality is often a weighty consideration influencing design choices.

Starting from the ground up, durable

This beloved King Charles spaniel is napping in a Directoire chair, newly reupholstered in Bennison Fabrics' linen rather than in his own toile-covered dog bed. Directoire style followed the French Revolution, which overturned the monarchy.

sisal rugs rest on hardwood floors, signaling an easygoing mood and lessening the seriousness of spaces. Humble seagrass, jute, and coir also loosen up formal rooms, making them more inviting. Although some Francophiles prefer bare floors, others are drawn to the beauty of hand-loomed oriental rugs that warm settings with color and texture—but mostly, the French prefer old Savonneries, which were once woven for royalty, and precious worn Aubussons with their tapestry-like weave. Always they lounge in privileged places in rooms with minimal traffic.

Shapely slipcovers that can be washed or dry-cleaned often protect seating with luxurious fabrics and impressive detailing hidden underneath. They also camouflage weary furniture, giving pieces a fresh look far less expensively than replacing or reupholstering. To their credit, slipcovers can quickly change the look of a room by echoing the season. When trees lose their leaves, chenilles, corduroys, and twills stand up to the cold. Come summer, furnishings shrug off these hearty wraps, leaving cool cottons and relaxed linens to lift the spirit of rooms.

At their intimate best, slipcovers fit sofas, chairs, and ottomans as perfectly as the chic evening gowns fit the Parisian women; they are as exquisitely tailored. Accoutrements, such as inverted pleating, scalloped hemlines, bow ties, and tucking over the arms, result from the fastidious care taken when laying out and cutting fabric. Contrasting welts, or flanges and trim, add a sophisticated air.

When it comes to upholstery, nailheads are common, supplying character and charm. The French, however, correctly point out that some American upholsterers space them too far apart at times, upsetting the proportions of even the best chairs.

Tellingly, French interiors say a great deal about the people who live in them, revealing their interests, tastes, and travels. Spaces brim with family portraits and photographs in frames, freshly cut flowers, old maps, and well-read books heaped high on coffee tables that are roomy enough to crowd drinks, hors d'oeuvres, accessories, and delicately scented lavender potpourri. Though settings appear to have come together in a natural way, rooms are extremely well thought out. Even the most modest things generally have a purpose. Sturdy side tables that withstand the rigors of playful, ever-present dogs offer places for drinks. Common features include decorative pillows, reading lights, warm throws, and seating that not only encourages bright conversation but also takes advantage of the view.

For the French, the new and the shiny hold no interest. Rather, spaces embrace treasured reminders of long ago that are central to their charm. Yet, there is no one specific look. Rooms are disarming repositories for an ever-growing blend of furnishings that indulge stylistic preferences. As each new generation comes up with its own version of French country— customizing settings with color and an eclectic harmony of old and new—the look is forever changing and unfolding, sometimes miles from its primitive past.

Early pieces continue to find new devoted audiences in Francophiles who see themselves as caretakers of the past, but there is even wider approval for old more-refined furnishings now that rural ways of life have nearly vanished.

With its broad stylistic range, interest in French country can be traced to 1610 when Louis XIII ascended the throne. Under his rule, the grand styles of furniture-making developed in each region based on skills, inspirations, and available woods.

In Provence, most furnishings were carved from walnut. However, a coterie of craftsmen fashioned pieces out of cherry, pear, and olive wood, too. Oak was the wood of choice for making prized armoires, buffets, and vaisseliers in the Normandy region of France, but many of the most soulful armoires were sculpted in the more malleable pine, and benches, tables, and chairs were carefully crafted in elm. Though some furniture was quite primitive, nearly all shared strong clean lines, massive proportions, elaborately turned posts, and somber geometric carvings, mainly diamonds and discs.

Radically different from the simplistic beauty of this early era were the flamboyance and excess that followed. During much of the baroque period—1643 to 1715—Louis XIV, the Sun King, ruled France from the magnificent Palace of Versailles. Opulent interiors, rife with heavily carved furniture, rich tapestries, regal tassels and fringe, and shimmering brocades, emerged suited to the king's extravagant image. Romantic frescoes—wall paintings on wet plaster—appeared at every turn, further reflecting his lavishness.

Tall ostentatious chairs with chunky upholstered backs and seats had straight legs that were either turned or carved with stretchers joining the legs in an X or figure eight. One needed a title, however, to appreciate the majesty of these chairs. Since only the self-indulgent king was allowed to sit in a *fauteuil*, or armchair, there were an abundance of stools and side chairs.

In an upward spiral of grandeur, the régence era—1700 to 1730 between the reigns of Louis XIV and Louis XV—gave way to a period that was ever more dazzling. Wood pieces radiated with carvings

of ribbons and foliage, the refined new embellishments. The *bombé,* or convex, commode made its debut. Cabriole legs began replacing straight ones. And, shapely curves were added to the upper sections of cabinets and bookcases.

Additionally, a fascination with the Far East that began in 1670, when the Trianon de Porcelaine at Versailles was built for one of Louis XIV's mistresses, increased. When demand for all things oriental—from silk screens and lacquered cabinets to blue-and-white porcelain vases and embroidered hangings—outstripped supply, French craftsmen copied these richly decorated pieces, some with gleaming varnished finishes, then added more

Napoleon laid costly Aubusson rugs, which came from the small village in central France of the same name, in each of his many residences. Preening swans and peacocks, foliage, and flowers embellished many of these tapestry-like weaves.

Aubussons, like all rugs of irresistible beauty, require proper care. Neglected masterpieces are occasionally cut into smaller pieces, then reworked into coveted pillows. Finding a cushion that coordinates with the hues in a room can be difficult, however, and sometimes prove expensive. The opulent pillows shown here are layered with trims complementing the living room's palette.

flourishes of their own. The look brought together Eastern inspiration and Western craftsmanship, creating the foundation for the style known as *chinoiserie*, which is still popular today.

Perhaps predictably, the régence era pointed the way for the more beguiling rococo period—1730 to 1760—when Louis XV and his mistress Madame de Pompadour had great influence on the decorative arts. Though public reception rooms retained their sense of glamour and grandeur, family apartments were refashioned into more intimate settings where strong colors were replaced with the pastels favored by Madame de Pompadour. The new formality embraced comfort. Louis XV sought inviting chairs rather than stools and fluid furniture arrange-

ments conducive to conversation.

As a result, the king's highly trained *menuisier*, or chairmaker, Jean-Baptiste Tilliard, sculpted a perfectly proportioned, low-curved armchair with an exposed wood frame far lighter and less regal-looking than any former chairs. On the seat rail of the *bergère*, he carved a basket of flowers. On its back, he shaped shells and *cartouches*, or unrolled scrolls, which communicated that this chair was not meant to stiffly line the wall but rather be moved about for spontaneous use.

As Parisian chairmakers began adopting Tilliard's designs, the frames of both caned and Louis XV bergère chairs were at times gilded or painted. Upholstered arms were moved back from the length of the seat so crinolines would

French Influences

Indisputably, creative freedom is what design is now about, safeguarding rooms from dull similarity. So why not turn your artistic energies into shaping a style that is at once appropriate for the space and uniquely your own? These suggestions may help.

♣ Take advantage of what is already in your home. A melting pot of furnishings can evoke the feeling of France, where pieces seldom match or take themselves so seriously that a room fails to be inviting. Teaming the unassuming with objects more grand adds spirit to settings when careful attention is paid to other details such as comfort and scale. When a room craves some French touches, let fabrics, baskets, and greenery suggest a European influence. Elegance does not automatically involve a huge investment, and a careful disarray can make a room look inviting and comfortable.

♣ Think imaginatively when arranging a room. Some of the most inviting settings are made up of pieces artfully set on an angle, floating in space and opening up the room. There need not be something in every corner, filling every inch, but an extra chair might be a welcome addition to your bedroom.

♣ Arrange a mix of similar objects on a commode or console. Furniture is only the start of a well-designed room. Accessories are important, too. Without them, settings look impersonal. Most groupings make a stronger statement when they are artfully made up of odd numbers—three plates on stands, or three old wooden boxes, five candlesticks varying in height. Whether parading pewter, brass, crystal, or silver, stay with the same medium for the greatest impact. Crowd picture frames together rather than scatter them around the room.

♣ Practice the French art of restraint when displaying things that are meaningful to you. Don't layer everything you own on one tabletop. Gently edit your belongings, aiming for a gracious mix of French and American style. Weave together something tall, something short, something old, something new, and something surprising, too, if possible.

♣ Buy the best you can afford. When need dictates, invest in a quality old piece or a finely crafted reproduction that is a faithful copy of an enduring design. Although an antique or two is essential for adding character and heritage to a room that might otherwise look too new, don't forget about well-made, well-worn secondhand reproductions that are superior to what you could purchase new, or vintage pieces that would look better painted.

♣ Spruce up a nondescript chest with some paint. The antique white-, gray-, green-, and soft aquamarine blue-painted furniture of Egyptian and oriental decorative artists so enchanted eighteenth-century French nobility that soon furniture surfaces all over Europe were being colorfully garnished.

♣ Rejuvenate tired hardwood floors by refinishing, painting, or stenciling them. Though hardwoods stand up better than carpet to the messes that pets can make, flooring need never be boring.

♣ Come up with an appealing wall arrangement by first laying out the grouping on the floor. An array of related prints hung closely together will be perceived as one homogeneous unit. In contrast, pictures, sconces, mirrors, and plates will lose their visual impact if hung too far apart. Also, consider propping pictures on shelves.

♣ Hang individual paintings at eye level, or if you are tall, a little higher. In rooms with eight-foot ceilings, hanging them five-feet-four inches from floor to the center often works. In rooms with higher ceilings, five-feet-five inches to the center is a more appealing height.

♣ Dress up important living spaces with rugs that fit your lifestyle. Wool yarns resist soiling and respond better to cleaning than man-made fibers. They also are inherently resistant to static and to flame. Long-wearing sisal is applauded for its versatility, but water can leave bleachlike blotches on some sisals. Don't overlook the appeal of sea grass. Unlike sisal, it does not react adversely to water. Sisal, jute, and sea-grass rugs are made from natural root fibers woven in a ropelike fashion. Generally, they are bound by rubber and finished with a latex bonding that makes for an easy glue-down installation in rooms where they are used wall to wall.

♣ Look to the French for direction, seeking fabrics with hues that blend rather than match. Florals, stripes, and checks can work together when the scales and the colors are compatible. You would not, for example, want a generous floral in the same room as a pin stripe. Nor would a strong floral look right with another large-scale pattern or with a mini-gingham check. Fabrics should balance each other. But it is also important for them to relate to the size and scale of the room. Chenilles are welcoming in rooms with high ceilings.

No one could accuse this upholsterer of placing these antique nailheads too far apart, nor could they criticize the way the Marvic pastoral toile is applied. The pattern is shown at its best on the designer's own French wing chairs in his richly furnished living room. Over the fireplace is an eighteenth-century French trumeau—a framed mirror, usually tall and rectangular, with a painted scene in a carved panel.

not be crushed. When hoop skirts were no longer in vogue, they would again extend forward, but always soft loose pillows rested on fabric-covered platforms and curvaceous legs remained stretcher-free. The rich damasks and velvets favored for upholstery would become hallmarks of this period.

Laborious carvings on other wood pieces were pulled from all aspects of nature, including shells, fish, waves, birds, vines, flowers, rocks, and serpents. Also, designs were commonly rooted in farming motifs such as corn and wheat. Ribbons with streamers and hearts became fashionable, too.

Furnishings were labeled Louis XIV, Louis XV, and later Louis XVI, though more often than not styles did not come into being during the reign of the king for whom they were named. Because the reign dates do not correspond to the style dates, it is more historically correct to instead say baroque, régence, rococo, and neoclassical.

For example, neoclassical began in 1765, years before the ascension of Louis XVI in 1774, and lasted until 1790. In rebellion against the overindulgence of baroque and rococo styles, curved legs were replaced by straight tapered ones, and shell and floral carvings were traded for urns and columns, lions' masks, and rams' heads. Parisian interiors generally embrace neoclassical or Louis XVI style.

As Americans mingle elegance and ease, the furnishings in many of their homes derive from the reign of Louis XV, relying on understated elegance for their charm. Some settings, however, rekindle a feeling of days gone by, borrowing from an even earlier time, placing more importance on rough-hewn finishes and eclectic pieces. Actually, the furnishings in American homes are extraordinarily varied,

drawing from a series of influences. Regardless, we commonly refer to rooms filled with Louis furniture as French country, correctly or incorrectly.

✤ TEXTILES ✤

The French are passionate about textiles. Since the seventeenth century, creating beautiful fabrics has been considered a medium of artistic expression in France, where old mills have endured despite the availability of less-expensive goods, and some looms are still producing new fabrics using age-old ways.

French *documents*—copies or adaptations of antique fabrics or wallpapers—are being reproduced in assorted new *colorways*—color schemes. Other designs grow from colors and textures. It is no secret, of course, that beyond furnishings, fabrics can instantly transform the character of a room. What may not be as commonly known is that the sun's damaging rays can readily destroy textiles. Fading or bleaching inevitably leads to fraying fibers, which results in shredding. Lining and interlining help guard fragile window treatments. In turn, curtains preserve upholstery from the ruin of harmful light.

Fiber—either natural or synthetic—is the origin of all fabrics. Natural fibers come from tufts of plants or animals and can be woven into cotton, linen, wool, and silk. Synthetics are the less-expensive laboratory-made fibers produced chemically, resulting in polyester, nylon, acrylic, rayon, and acetate. They are generally stronger and more resistant to fading from the sun than natural fibers. Also, they resist wrinkling, but they tend to droop and pill. Before selecting a fabric, it is wise to consider where it will be used, the amount of wear to which it will be subjected, and its care. To wrap an elegant

Dye lots vary, so it's best always to request a cutting for approval when ordering fabric to verify the goods are within an acceptable color range. In addition, repeats sometimes differ by an inch or two from the showroom samples, so one must not skimp on fabric. Some fabrics can be railroaded, meaning they can be applied horizontally across a sofa or other upholstered piece rather than vertically, thereby eliminating obvious seams.

living room in suitable splendor, for example, silks, damasks, and velvets might be appropriate. In a family room cottons or textures might be a better choice.

Perhaps more than any others, two fabrics have long been tied to the French. Toiles de Jouy prints originated in the mid-eighteenth century at the Oberkampf factory in the French town of Jouy-en-Josas, near Versailles. Monochrome prints, usually red or blue on white cotton or muslin ground, depicted pastoral- and mythological-etched scenes. Later, toiles illustriously celebrated current events, including the first balloon trip, the American struggle for independence, and

the French Revolution. Authentically French, they are still highly sought, both here and abroad, for use in important living spaces as well as bedrooms.

During the seventeenth century, the French began producing *indiennes,* decorative block-printed cottons that were once imported from India. For years, these Provençal mini-flowers—more generous florals, paisleys, and medallions—highlighted in color-drenched hues, presented such strong competition for the silk and wool textile mills owned by the Crown that they finally were banned in French provinces. For a while, this only succeeded in making them even more desired, and

$\mathcal{A}$ Nina Campbell striped coverup is set to welcome sunny afternoons. The tea-stained pillow is dressed in a vintage fabric and lace. When days grow shorter, French dressing calls for layering a brick red Marvic toile and Bennison pillow with Brunschwig & Fils loop fringe. Of course, not all fabrics make ideal slipcovers. Avoid synthetics, which attract dirt, and heavy fabrics that drape poorly.

Fabric Facts

When shopping for textiles it is helpful to know a little about the characteristics of those you are considering, as well as some terms associated with fabrics.

✤ Backing—is a coating applied to give fabric more strength and stability. Acrylic backing is used both for upholstery and wall applications. Knit backing is commonly used for upholstery and draperies.

✤ Batiste—is a fine filmy fabric, named for the French weaver Jean Batiste, usually made using only the choicest cotton yarns.

✤ Brocade—has a rich raised design, often of stylized flowers, that resembles embroidery. Traditionally made of silk, originally in gold and silver, it is often available today in cotton and cotton blends. For extra strength, it often requires backing before being used on upholstery.

✤ Chenille—is French for "caterpillar"; its soft fuzzy yarns make it a perfect choice for fringes, tassels, and upholstery. It does, however, have a propensity to unravel, especially when seams are skimpy. To avoid this, designers have a light latex backing applied before shipping to upholstery workrooms. Throw-pillow fabric need not be backed.

✤ Chintz—is a cotton fabric printed with bold flowers, birds, or fruits, and often glazed or treated with a resin finish that creates a soft sheen known to repel dirt. It is ideal for upholstery and window treatments.

✤ Corduroy—is a heavy cotton or synthetic fabric with evenly spaced ridges, or wales, running the length of the fabric.

✤ Cotton—is made from fibers of the boll of the cotton plant, which are spun and woven into a fabric with infinite uses. Quality is determined by the length of the fibers, which can vary from less than one-half inch to more than two inches—the longer being the better. Durable yet soft, it is appropriate for both window treatments and upholstery.

✤ Damask—is a weave that dates back to the thirteenth century, alternating satin and matte to create a reversible fabric. Introduced in Europe by Marco Polo and named for the city of Damascus, Damassé is French for "damask." It is suitable for draperies, upholstery, and table linens.

✤ Finish—is the treatment given to produce napping, embossing, glazing, waterproofing, or wrinkle resistance.

✤ Gingham—is a cotton or synthetic fabric printed in one color on white, creating a check.

❖ Hand—is the softness, firmness, and elasticity of a fabric, or how it feels. Its resilience, flexibility, and drapability are influenced by its finish.

❖ Jacquard—is fabric woven on a Jacquard loom that uses perforated cards to create intricate patterns. Damasks, tapestries, and brocades are woven this way.

❖ Linen—is a strong yarn produced from flax that can be woven into fabric. Slubs, which are swollen fibers, are inherent in the yarn, but they are not flaws. For all linen's beauty, it lacks elasticity, which results in wrinkles. It is wise to have it backed before using it for upholstery. Linen is often blended with cotton.

❖ Matelassé—is a soft fabric that appears quilted and is produced by weaving two sets of warp and weft threads on a Jacquard loom. Once used primarily for blanket covers, it is now used for window treatments and upholstery as well.

❖ Moiré—is a ribbed fabric—often silk, acetate, or taffeta—with wavy watermarks produced by engraving rollers.

❖ Muslin—is a weightless, gauzy cotton fabric often used for curtains and bed hangings.

❖ Ottoman—is a heavy, stiffly ribbed fabric with silk warp and cotton weft.

❖ Sheer—is a thin translucent fabric, such as lace or muslin, used for window treatments and bed draping.

❖ Silk—is the most beautiful of all fibers, and may be woven alone or blended with other natural or synthetic fibers. It has a fine hand, drapes gracefully, and absorbs dyes well, so it can be richly colored in jewel-like tones. Silk also is fragile and readily destroyed by strong sunlight. Before using for upholstery, it requires knit backing, which gives the textile added strength.

❖ Taffeta—is a woven fabric with subtle ribbing and silky texture.

❖ Tapestry—is a heavy woven fabric originally used just for hangings, now also used for upholstery.

❖ Twill—is a durable fabric with a diagonal grain, produced by weft yarns passing over one or more warp threads, then under two or more warp yarns. Herringbone, denim, and gabardine are woven in this manner.

❖ Wool—is a natural fiber produced from the fleece of animals, usually sheep.

❖ Velvet—is a soft luxurious fabric with a short dense pile.

❖ Warp—is a set of fixed yarns that run the length of the loom. Interlacing, or weaving weft and warp yarns that alternate each row, produces a fabric.

❖ Weft—is a set of fixed threads that run across the loom.

the mill in Tarascon, outside Avignon, secretly continued to produce the indiennes, but then interest fell. When Charles Deméry took responsibility for the factory in 1933, it was making only cotton scarves. First, he set about correcting misdeeds, then he renamed the mill Souleiado. Pierre Deux brought these vegetable-died fabrics to the United States where they found their way to the White House and into our public rooms.

❧ WINDOW DRESSINGS ❧

Window treatments can diffuse light, guard privacy, and screen awkward views, but at their splendid best, they are artistic inspirations. With or without the trimmings, or *la passementerie*—fringes, tassels, cording, tiebacks, tapes, and braids—curtains can add the chic finishing touch to any room.

Window treatments hang more luxuriously and look more dramatic when one does not skimp on fabric. For elegant curtains, measure two-and-a-half to three times the finished width. When working with sheers—lace, voile, organdy, muslin, and batiste—or gauzy fabrics that drape softly, tripling the width will help insure privacy. Extending the curtains twelve to fifteen inches on each side of the window not only preserves natural light but also produces a more alluring look. It is important, however, to respect the scale and proportions of the room while increasing the sense of space.

Linings are always necessary with window treatments. A hidden interlining will add body, creating an even richer professional look. Both will help prevent the sun from bleaching fabrics. Many designers use heavy dense fabric as lining to block the light. Of course, when working with loosely woven gauzy fabrics a lining is not necessary.

The most dramatic curtains puddle on the floor, invariably creating an inviting spot for the dog to stretch out and fall asleep. For this reason, pet owners often prefer that their curtains simply brush the floor. Those that stop short have an unesthetic, almost imbalanced, appearance. In addition, operable curtains hang more gracefully when weights are sewn into the hems.

Welts, fringes, braiding, and tape often produce sophisticated window treatments. Piping, too, can give curtains an edge. One of the most influential tastemakers of the twentieth century, Sister Parish, said, "Curtains must always have an edge or an ending."

Curtains should be hung as close to the ceiling as possible to heighten the feeling of a room. In rooms with high ceilings and beautiful millwork, install them approximately two inches below the crown molding. In France, curtains often hang from simple iron rails. Tasteful hardware is a meaningful part of any window treatment.

Sill-length treatments are less dressy than flowing curtains. Shades can be dressed up or dressed down in untold ways to fit the most casual or formal settings.

The designer's celebrated workroom hand-pleated these deep goblets, meticulously centering the brown stripe in each. Contrasting brown rope tacked to the front of each goblet creates added interest while stunning brown-and-metallic-gold oversized tassels decoratively tie back the curtains and help capture the grandeur of the room.

*T*op dealers willingly share the history of their pieces. This intricately carved eighteenth-century walnut armoire unearthed in Provence is upholstered in Travers's Melton Squares, thereby preventing table linens from snagging. Double welting outlines the doors and shelving.

To make the most of an unassuming space, the designer drew inspiration from chinoiserie. The framed painting, however, is not quite what it seems. Instead, it is trompe l'oeil, a delightful deception or illusion. An antique commode is indeed fitted with modern plumbing.

Bookcases span the library walls, creating deep-set windows and perfect niches for high-backed wing chairs, but beyond the generously scaled furniture and tapestry fabrics—the earliest were made in Paris during the fourteenth century—there is a sense of the lives lived here. Stacks of old magazines, back issues of medical journals, tabbed books, and a sprawling dog—all unseen—reflect the designer and her husband's interests.

*W*ith graceful curves, hand-carving, and a radiant claret-and-gold Creation Baumann check, this Louis XV bergère chair casts its own light on European style. Flanging on the seat cushion adds sophistication. Elsewhere in the room, where there is meticulous attention to detail, fabrics are layered with assurance.

❧

*W*ith its comfortable chairs and scholarly air, this library provides a cozy spot where the home owner, who is also the designer, can visit with friends, enjoy dinner in front of the fireplace, or scheme rooms. The sofa, covered in a Brunschwig & Fils toile, is one of many spots for reading.

Engaging fabrics meet on a quilted window seat with layers of pillows. Flanges are bias cut with knotted or gathered corners.

A landscape of Pierre Deux fabrics gathers around a mellow breakfast table that has become swaybacked from all the years of use. Parsons chairs have fresh, scalloped slipcovers. A 1930s Paris designer at the Parson School of Design came up with the basic look of the chairs, which are modified here.

Fine painted furniture, regally finished, had its beginnings in China about 3,500 years ago, but its legacy lingers today.

Ultimately it is the objets d'art that fill a room and make it personal. Placed carefully on a console table is an impressive array of tortoise-shell objects selectively collected over time.

*A*n eye for detail is evident in this living room that proves French country at its most sophisticated recognizes the need for comfort and conversational practicality. While the old and new mingle happily, melon walls provide a dramatic backdrop for a Patterson Flynn & Martin custom-colored rug, a charming Clarence House leopard print, and intriguing antiques.

French-country living has long been centered in the kitchen, so the French devote much thought to creating warm inviting rooms where family and friends can

Table MATTERS

happily gather and pets can roam freely. However, France is also the renowned gastronomic capital of the world, which means culinary standards necessitate planning kitchens that are functional, too. ⚜ Though traditional French kitchens are as distinctive as the souffles and béarnaise sauces made in them, all are amazingly efficient. Which is to say, that there is almost an alarming array of *batterie de cuisine*, or equipment, designed to steam, strain, boil, and drain, within easy reach and in full view. ⚜ Scores of heavy

Inarguably this kitchen owes a helping of its charm to the ultimate gourmet range—the La Cornue, which has been produced in France since 1908. A center island offers extra work space for serious cooks who revel in serving classic French cuisine. This is not to suggest that you must be a connoisseur to recognize good taste.

old copper pots, pans, and bowls in grad-
uating sizes crowd ceilings, hanging out
for all to see on pot racks, or *crémaillères*,
which are an integral part of almost every
space. In copper, sauces and gravies heat
quickly and evenly at low temperatures,
then rapidly cool. Also, egg whites whip to
their greatest heights in unlined copper
bowls. Since authentic French kitchens do
not have upper cabinets, open shelving
allows ready access to pottery, glassware,
platters, and trays—or any other pieces
needed.

Whereas Americans tend to hide
clutter in the pantry, in France old wire
baskets used for storing eggs and serving
crusty breads chaotically vie for counter
space with collections of tin molds—some
for baking, some for chocolate making,
and some for ice cream. Countertops also
burst with dozens of utensils for every
imaginable purpose. Windowsills boast
mossy pots of rosemary, thyme, sage, and
fennel used in cooking, which is an everyday pleasure.

Whether a simple family lunch, an
afternoon tea, or dinner with close friends,
presentation counts. The French table is a
perennially pleasing landscape of personal
taste that is set with as much care and love
as the food served upon it.

Tables are topped with fine damask
cloths or once-extraordinarily-expensive
lace cloths that are artfully showcased with
pastel underskirts highlighting their
detailed delicate patterns. On relaxed occasions, bright Provençal prints add a dash of
fun, or linens fittingly suit a bistro mood.

An unpretentious blend of artistically
combined dinnerware suggests the degree
of formality linked with an event. Mixing
patterns is common. Many families gather
silver, porcelain, and brightly colored
faïence—a chunky practical earthenware—

*The French have long inspired American chefs, even if some of us have not yet
matched their talents. But the high-tech appliances in our kitchens often put those
abroad to shame. Still, earnest cooks on both sides of the Atlantic prize copper cook-
ware, which effeciently handles routine tasks.*

from flea markets, so settings that find
their way to tables can be relatively inexpensive. In the early eighteenth century,
faïence was generally blue on white. Today,
an array of sun-washed glazes are available
with the most notable new additions—
marigold and emerald.

The French are also adept at making
beautiful glasses in various shapes, styles,
and sizes. Though the main meal of the
day—the midday repast—is always accom-
panied by wine, stemmed wine glasses are
reserved for special occasions. Sturdy

Christopher Hyland's soft linen curtains caress a window that floods the room with light. Elegant pewter buttons add an artful element to chairs covered in a Provençal print. Nearby stands an eighteenth-century armoire, offering a glimpse of pewter, mostly vintage, but some produced in this century. Meanwhile, nineteenth-century prints charmingly line the wall.

chunky tumblers are used daily for both water and wine.

✤ FOOD FOR THOUGHT ✤

Most American want their kitchens to function efficiently and to be equipped with the latest state-of-the-art appliances, but rather than sacrifice old-fashioned charm, we hide refrigerators and dishwashers behind panels that match our cabinets. Today the look of old cabinetry, moldings, and floor treatments is readily duplicated. Far from disguised, however, is the trend toward commercial-looking appliances,

which began with ranges and now includes heavy-duty dishwashers. Thanks to improved technology, the new brushed finish on stainless steel keeps fingerprints and scratches from showing and is far easier to care for. As a result, stainless steel is giving black appliances, and white, too, some stiff competition for kitchen space.

✤ TILE ✤

Almost without exception, every French kitchen has some trace of tile. In some, tiles fit together like pieces of a puzzle creating a mural. However, a beautifully

Creating a French Country Kitchen

Regardless, now that homey kitchens are no longer limited to rag rugs, dried flowers, and rooster prints, many creative ways to give a space a French twist still abound. Of course, installing a beamed ceiling and center island with a pot rack overhead will accomplish the task, and so will punctuating the room with tile. Also, a sizable farm table, Louis XV banquettes, an armoire, and some lace curtains can readily add a French touch. The following is a list of suggestions that are even easier.

❧ Hang a pleasing mix of old ceramic plates or platters on a breakfast-room wall, using the simple spring-tension wire hangers that are available. The plates will capture attention no matter where you put them, but the kitchen soffit is also an eye-pleasing spot.

❧ If you opt for wallcovering in a kitchen with a soffit, choose one with a small or medium-sized repeat—the distance from the point the pattern begins to the point it begins duplicating itself. A paper with a large repeat, say twenty-three to thirty inches, will look odd unless there is a nearby wall where you can see the full pattern.

❧ Textured walls suggest vintage charm, but with glazing you can convincingly replicate aging on flat wallboard. For fun, also think about stenciling a favorite saying on a soffit or wall. One particularly clever saying is "If You Accept a Dinner Invitation, You Have a Moral Obligation to be Amusing." —The Duchess of Windsor.

❧ Revive tired-looking wood cabinet doors with a coat of fresh paint. Afterwards, spice up panels and drawers with hand painting that picks up the hues of fabrics in the room. Then trade old hinges for new hidden ones, and replace worn knobs and pulls. When individual cabinet doors are truly not salvageable, think about having new ones milled to match the originals, or give your kitchen a French touch by removing a few of the worst doors, showing off pottery and bowls on open shelves.

❧ Highlight collections on counters with under-cabinet lights. Let a mixer in a bold shade of red, green, or blue add a dash of color. Paint the kitchen blue. Legend has it that the French, like people in other Mediterranean countries, once believed that blue could guard against evil spirits. With hopes of keeping all manner of misfortune away, not only were kitchens painted blue but also the trim around windows and doors.

❧

*S*ome tiles arrived lauding glorious French wines and cuisine. On those once blank, the designer suggested hand-painting the names of some of the owner's favorite French stops— a glorious château in the Loire Valley, the Hôtel de Crillion in Paris, with its luxurious Louis XVI furnishings and polished parquet floors, overlooking the regal Place de la Concorde, and Taillevent, a restaurant for serious gourmets, located in the posh eighth arrondissement.

*W*hen shopping for terracotta floor tiles, the selection is vast. Rectangles, hexagons, and squares can be mixed and laid in intricate patterns, mirroring the past. The reclaimed tiles from France shown here have the patina of age.

A Francophile at heart, the designer brings a taste of France into his newly re-modeled Tulsa, Oklahoma, kitchen. Everyday dishes sit conveniently on open shelves while canisters fill the counters in a relaxed way. Bovine collectibles hint at a passion for animals.

An array of distinctive French accents, worn by time, gently reminds us of a simpler way of life a century ago.

tiled backsplash is the focal point of most country kitchens.

The range of tiles varies from common glossy white to delicately painted faïence to those with natural irregularities in endless shapes and sizes. The unevenness of color typical of handmade pieces only adds to its charm. For a salvaged look, some tiles are glazed with an impervious glass-like finish that looks much like spider webbing, but mostly it is unglazed terra-cotta tiles that create the flavor of France. In regions where clay is plentiful—Provence, Burgundy, and the Loire Valley—oversized squares, octagons, and plain fields outlined with coordinating borders are common flooring. Elsewhere, black-and-white checkerboard floors are popular, too.

✤ D I N I N G   I N   ✤

The French dining room is a welcoming place, offering a stirring feast for the eye and the appetite. Handsome wood pieces with well-worn patinas and beautiful dinnerware—china, cut crystal, flatware, and silver—look as if they have served generations of family and friends. A glimmering chandelier makes the room glow, with an assortment of candlesticks contributing to the mood.

As one might expect, no table is complete without flowers, but no longer are arrangements light and airy. These days, sumptuous, tightly massed, overscaled bunches of the same fresh-cut flower or like-colored monochromatic blooms are being favored over more complex arrangements.

In our current mode, we like centerpieces that give guests something to talk about the day after a dinner party. As a result, some hostesses are embellishing their tables with garden tools, urns, and small treasures unearthed from vintage trunks.

Suggestions for Laying Tile

✤ If you are in the market for new tile, let home centers and showroom vignettes spark your creativity by offering suggestions for applications. Take along fabric, paint, and wood samples, along with any drawings that will help in coordinating your needs. Having a realistic estimate of your budget will also help.

✤ Even on a small budget, ceramic tile can have a big impact when you plan carefully. For pizzazz, intersperse a few handpainted tiles among a field of plain tiles on a backsplash where they are sure to be noticed.

✤ Oversize floor tiles can make a room seem larger, especially when tiles are laid on the diagonal, pulling the eye to each far-reaching corner. In contrast, small tiles in cramped quarters can make an area appear even smaller. To avoid a busy feeling, which can be visually stifling, use large-scale tile on the floor and a smaller-scale coordinating tile on counters and walls.

✤ Place tiles close together, then fill joints between tiles with a grout color that closely matches the tile. Tight grout lines will help create the feeling of spaciousness. Unglazed tiles can be protected against stains by using a nonporous epoxy grout or by applying a penetrating sealer once a cement-based grout is in place. Mortar—a mixture of cement, sand, and water, and, at times, lime—is used as a setting bed when installing tiles. If remodeling, keep in mind that tile may raise slightly the height of an existing floor. As a result, adjoining rooms may require new doorsills.

✤ To allow for breakage and oddly shaped rooms, order approximately 10 percent more tile than required. In the bathroom, always start with a full tile at the top center of the tub wall. Usually this is the spot where your eye travels first.

For some time, Americans have been longing for dining chairs that are comfortable, which means arms are helpful. Eighteenth-century French chairs are too shallow and too narrow for guests to linger at the table. Nineteenth-century chairs were larger scale, and, as a result, they are more inviting. By dressing chairs in slipcovers, it is possible to add warmth to dining rooms that have more than their share of hard surfaces. Of course, curtains can help, too.

People often wonder how large a chandelier should be to look as though it belongs in a setting. One rule of thumb to determine an appropriate size is to add the length and width of the room, then change the word feet to inches. For example, if the room measures fifteen feet long and thirteen feet wide, hang a chandelier that is approximately twenty-eight inches in diameter. Another suggests measuring the width of the room, doubling it, then again converting this number to inches for the correct diameter, in this case twenty-six inches. Either method will work, and knowing both methods allows for flexibility.

✤ THE FINE ART OF SERVING WINES ✤

Selecting a fitting wine to complement a meal can be mystifying enough without coming up with the right stemware. This doesn't mean there is just one right glass for a given wine, but the glass shape can greatly affect the taste of a fine wine.

Wines originate from hundreds of varieties of grapes, but only a few dozen kinds are long-standing favorites that determine the flavors for thousands of different wines. To taste all the flavors that a fine bottle of wine has to offer, enthusiasts suggest one style of glass for champagne or sparkling wines, another for white wines, and a third for red wines.

A glass for red wine should be larger and rounder than a glass for white wine. The thickness of the glass makes a difference, too. Preferably it should have a smooth rim with no lip. Colored and opaque glasses or those with a design should be avoided. Only colorless glasses allow one to see the clarity of the wine. A glass foot that is as wide as the widest part of the bowl produces a glass that is stable.

The stem of any wineglass should be long enough to comfortably grasp. Then one can easily give the wine a swirl to release its aroma without holding the glass by the bowl. Doing so alters the temperature and disrupts the balance of the wine, so when tasting wine, it is important to hold the glass correctly—by the stem instead of the bowl.

For champagne, use narrow elegant flutes to keep the bubbles from quickly dissipating. A glass for white wine should hold six ounces when two thirds full. It should feel paper-thin when one sips, meaning it should not have a rim. A slightly bowl-shaped glass enhances the fruit. Ideally, a glass for red wine should also hold six ounces when half full. A balloon-shaped bowl allows plenty of room for the wine's aroma to gather in the space above. Also, once in the glass, a wine needs to breathe, so a wineglass should never be filled to the brim. In addition, wineglasses are usually set up right to left and poured in this direction.

This wine cellar boasts an enviable collection of carefully chosen wines from noted vintners, making matching foods and wines less of a challenge. Although most Americans follow the old rule—red wine with meat and white wine with poultry and fish—the French drink red wine with all but seafood. Also, they attribute their low rate of coronary heart disease to quaffing down wine with meals.

Wrapped in windows, this breakfast room with bare floors and a rich palette of blues would look right at home in the south of France. Fresh bagels serve as napkin rings, adding charm to the morning meal.

*T*aken by the charm of nineteenth-century stained-glass windows sitting in an antique shop, the designer could not resist toting them home. With accents of blue, they fit right into a space where it is necessary to mask the view, making a window inappropriate. Still, they invite light into the kitchen, just as her practiced eye told her they would.

A sunshine yellow charger highlights Italian pottery set for a midday brunch. Also helping to create a well-dressed tabletop is the bead-edged plate and bowl. When it comes to flowers, "Let nature be your teacher," suggests the poet William Wordsworth. The most appealing groupings look almost—but not quite—as if the flowers were just gathered from the garden and effortlessly arranged.

A glass-top table creates the illusion of roominess in a small area where there is always space for family. Aside from its good looks, this table offers the advantage of easy cleanups after little people color and paint.

A whirlwind makeover transformed this once timeworn kitchen and gloomy laundry room into a bright, sumptuous space that includes color-washed walls, hand-hewn timbers, and a vaulted ceiling.

In this multicultural kitchen, canisters from Italy offer smart storage. Cabinets are glazed white oak.

*C*omplete with a commercial range, suspended pot rack, and admirable tile, this well-equipped kitchen shares its enthusiasm for cooking. The sink overlooks a garden of flowers that celebrates the French style.

Inspired by the picturesque countryside, decorative tile embraces counters and climbs walls, capturing the allure of France. Colorful borders add interest, leading the way for a smooth transition between smaller and larger, bolder tiles.

Exuding Provençal style, the focal point of this kitchen is the attractive hood. Here, French tag tiles slide into drawer fronts, lending European authenticity.

𝒯he hand-painted dining-room walls, glazed green chairs, and mix of pottery exude lighthearted French style. While the curtains are stunning in their simplicity—with a simple moss green grosgrain ribbon set back and flowing down the panel's leading edge—the hardware plays a starring role in the window treatment. The antique curtain rings are brass with unusual designs. Though the finials give the illusion of being old, they are new. The chandelier forged in France has long been in the family.

*H*and-molded faïence plates gathered in Paris flea markets each have a different pattern. Wide-mouth confit pots grouped together also are old. Today, most new pots are manufactured in Spain.

A wine cellar in the pantry floor stocks both French and American wines, with glassware—from water to wine to champagne—nearby.

A table overlooking a brilliant garden is set for a casual family breakfast. It showcases MacKenzie-Childs, Ltd. enamelware plates, which are kiln-fired and hand-painted in various designs. The birdcage has the attention of a cat wandering in and out.

In her own kitchen, the author displays a passion for orderliness. A parade of French faïence farm animals offer a playful distraction from meal planning. Hand-textured walls, color-washed in taupe, add layers of age. The French limestone floor has eased edges. The pewter hardware garnishing the mahogany cabinets is also from France.

The family's newest additions fill some of the frames lighting up breakfast-room shelves. Though these pewter frames are from Portugal, both the table linens and hand-painted magnolia porcelain embellishing the table are American made.

To keep the morning sun from intruding, the designer melded shades and curtain panels in subtle prints. Traditionally pots de confit were used in the south of France for preserving duck or goose for cassoulet. The bottom halves were left unglazed to keep the contents cool when the pots were buried halfway in the ground. Today these old jars sporting cracks and chips of time are prized.

Painting is the quickest way to brighten a space, but hand-painting cabinets, drawers, and the refrigerator can add even more personality. Stepping into this kitchen gives one the feeling of actually being in Provence.

In a dining room that abounds with antiques, there is a sense of comforting richness. A winterscape with delicate shading hangs above a deep fireplace with masterful lines. Like the fireplaces in chic European homes, the one shown here has an impressive mantel and surround.

$\mathcal{S}$ure to capture even the most casual observer's attention is the antique hand-painted majolica that reveals the owners' respect for the past. Picking up on nature's motifs and hues, these prized plates boast the crackle finish characteristic of hand-made majolica, which dates back to the thirteenth century when Italian artisans first adopted this craft from Moorish potters.

In a house built for entertaining, three sixty-inch round tables are more conducive to conversation than one large rectangular one. Imported Louis XV armchairs gather round. When a dinner party isn't on the calendar, plywood tables are elegantly swaddled in the same Cowtan & Tout silk as the windows. In keeping with the scale of the room, oversized tassels catch the dramatic celedon-and-cream curtains, which puddle opulently on the floor. The handsome linen area rug is from France.

*A*live with the scent of fresh blooms, the table is beautifully set with gleaming Buccellati silver, exquisite hand-painted porcelain from Herend, and breathtaking crystal from the luxury French house Saint Louis.

*S*hunning the grandeur of anything more studied, this charming, rustic breakfast room with timber ceiling and brick floors opens to a contented kitchen that is perfect for after-school get-togethers. Faïence finds from France decorate the table.

*A*n unexpected alcove with checkerboard walls, banquettes, and café tables is perfect for enjoying wine and cheese as the evening unfolds. Guests can move to the quiet of a telephone booth to take or make a call on an old-fashioned phone readied with a touch-tone keypad and tone/pulse dialing. Nearby, a covered patio is outfitted for outdoor entertaining.

For centuries, the bedroom was where high-level meetings took place until Louis XV's renowned mistress Madame de Pompadour—the arbiter of eighteenth-century taste—removed it from the list

Bedrooms, BEDDING, AND BATHS

of public rooms. Her example was followed by all of Europe's privileged class, then pervaded all social classes. After that, the bedroom became worthy of being called a *boudoir,* which in French means a "private retreat." ⚜ Regardless, the French lavish extraordinary attention on their beds with sensuous linens, cozy comforters, and *traversins*—bolsters supporting generous layers of pillows. Canopied beds billow romantically in silk, linen, or gauzy fabrics with airy weaves, now that bed hangings no longer

Beautifully painted furniture is a hallmark of eighteenth-century French style. Yet here, fine craftsmanship and artistic wizardry fool the eye into believing what is new is old. The bed, chest, and chair were crafted in Italy for Atlanta-based Patina, whose mission is re-creating fine painted furniture.

must fend off drafts in poorly heated rooms. Popular, too, are the flowery prints of Provence and authentic Toiles de Jouy fabrics, which convey the unmistakably sophisticated mood that is so distinctly French.

In noble circles, the bed was a symbol of family wealth and social status. So, not unexpectedly, the bed of Louis XIV was as admirable as his throne. The tall posts were richly dressed with elaborate tassels and exquisitely carved fluted finials. Which is not to say that all beds were as grand. Some were merely imposing. Others were small, chunky, and uncomfortable.

Today, the French boudoir is as likely to be used for corresponding as for sleeping, so it typically includes a writing table. Although precious Aubusson rugs still grace many rooms; bare floors are also common. Seldom do the French lay carpet.

The armoire forever remains the essential French-country piece. Originally used in thirteenth-century France to store armor (hence, its name), it soon became a necessity for housing an entire family's clothes, food, and other sparse possessions. Often it was a wedding present from parents who had received it as a wedding present. Interestingly, closets were born in the twentieth century.

❧ THE MASTER BEDROOM ❧

On American shores, one-third of our lives are spent sleeping. However, we, too, no longer think of the bedroom simply as a place to rest. Instead, the master bedroom has become the spot to recharge from life on the run—the perfect hideaway from the responsibility for meals, meetings, even the children. It reflects our growing need for a getaway where we can spread out the newspaper, listen to music,

watch television, or curl up with a good book. For some, it also doubles as a creative workspace or home office.

However, to qualify as a true personal sanctuary, the bed must not be the only place to sit. There needs to be another comfortable spot for laboring away on a trusty laptop, struggling with the crossword puzzle in Sunday's *New York Times*, or having a sandwich.

To create a snug intimate haven that gently lifts our spirits, we need to put to rest any old ideas of matching beds, dressers, and chests of drawers. Instead we need to think of surrounding ourselves with a mix of pieces old and new, a chaise lounge, artwork, whatever we love. Shapes, patterns, and textures can harmoniously play off one another. Then, taking a cue from the French, the bed becomes the focal point.

Few beds are more romantic than a canopy bed swathed in fabric. However,

W̶hat could be more glorious than starting the day with a fresh croissant and the newspaper in the comfort of bed? The Royal Limoges breakfast set is made especially for Oustau de Baumanière, a grand hôtel in the French town of les Baux. Bedding from Frette, the Italian manufacturer renowned for heirloom quality linens, has embroidered silk-organza trim, emitting a European air.

Sunshine streams through the skylight onto the grouping of irresistible old vanity jars with precious sterling tops in this master bathroom. The trinket box dates back to the nineteenth century. Sterling frames, both old and new, were collected in the owner's travels. Gleaming brass fixtures are from Waterworks in Danbury, Connecticut. For the mirrors and sconces, Oakland, California-based Ironies bent iron into organic forms such as twigs, leaves, and kumquats.

neither a canopy nor a bulky four-poster bed is necessarily the best choice in a small bedroom or one with a low ceiling. Even though a canopy can create old-world charm in a room devoid of architectural detailing, it is easy for the canopy and a four-poster to dominate a room. If a four-poster is used in a room with a low ceiling, a bed with slender pencil-thin posts that visually doesn't intrude on air space is preferable. When the bed has pretty side rails, exposed legs can help heighten the feeling of a room.

Additionally, a sleigh bed should not be crammed into limited space. Despite its dramatic appeal, its design adds inches to the length. First crafted after the French Revolution in 1789, which toppled the monarchy and brought Napoleon Bonaparte into power, the sleigh bed still remains a classic that calls for spacious rooms.

Among the choices that often work well in rooms of any size are hand-painted beds, iron beds, and steel beds. Many new beds are too low. Ideally, the box springs

Changing the Mood of Your Bedroom

✤ Rearrange the furniture. Before moving everything, it helps to draft a detailed floor plan to find out exactly how much work space you have. You will need some one-inch-to-the-foot graph paper for drawing the room to scale. First, measure the space, including windows, doorways, and vents. Blocking heating and air conditioning openings can trap the air and affect climate control adversely. Next, measure the furnishings and cut out shapes representing these pieces. Try numerous layouts, including angling your bed in a corner. Not all furniture need be set perpendicular or parallel to the walls. Finally, analyze your options. A bedroom looks best when the bed is the focal point and the headboard is the first thing you see upon entering the room, but this is not always possible.

✤ Move in a desk, chest, or chair from another room. If space is tight, place the desk next to the bed where it can also function as a nightstand. Otherwise, try placing it perpendicular to a window. A chest of drawers can also serve as a bed table while providing extra storage. If possible, float an upholstered chair away from a corner, then let a small book table, pole lamp, and magazine basket complete the composition. Conserve floor space by stacking treasured books under the table. Paint or wallcovering are also easy ways to change the personality of a room. Later either can easily become the base for a palette. Meanwhile, let pillows add a dash of color.

✤ Fill in a gap with a new plant in a large basket. Redo your closet, including shelves. Hang some family pictures in a grouping. Fill picture frames with recent family photos, and put some lavender in your room.

✤ When starting from scratch or redoing a room, choose three fabrics that work together—perhaps a print, check, and stripe. For the tableskirt choose a fabric that stands out a little from the bedskirt, and for the bedskirt, select a fabric that differs from the coverlet. The bedskirt fabric is often a good choice for the back of shams, sham flanges, and the window treatment.

⚜

Restoring peace of mind is easy in the comfort of this romantic boudoir with salmon walls, pleasing patterns, and silk-ribbon fringe. The two-drawer chest is hand-painted with acanthus leaves, a centuries-old decorative symbol. A chaise tucked in the corner invites relaxing with a good book.

should be set up twelve inches from the floor, so that one must ascend into the bed rather than tumble down onto it. Raising a bed to a new height can be accomplished by laying two-by-fours under the box springs along the bed frame. The easy addition of lumber brings a low-slung bed to a more attractive height. Beds resplendent of the past generally require a twenty-one-inch European-length bedskirt.

✤ BEDDING ✤

Most sheets available in the United States have thread counts—the number of threads per woven square inch—falling between 120 and 380. A few collections offer heirloom-quality 560-thread-count linens, but these are mostly for the table. It is generally thought that the higher the thread count, the more extravagant and softer the sheeting, but relying strictly on thread count can be misleading. The fibers used can make a drastic difference in the softness, density, and drape of a sheet.

Pure cotton is the most popular bedding; however, pure linen sheets are arguably more highly prized since linen is one of the longest-lasting natural fibers. Its peerless beauty is unique because the more linen sheeting is used and washed, the softer, stronger, and more supple the fabric becomes. In short, it improves with age. Also linen sheeting is mildew and moth resistant, nonstatic, and lint-free. Clearly more costly than cotton bedding, properly laundered linen sheeting promises to last for decades. Linen does, however, require more care.

✤ GUEST BEDROOMS ✤

The French have always loved entertaining guests, from those who come for dinner to weary travelers who stay for weeks. Americans also have turned pampering house guests into an art form, heralding back to a time when people lived far apart and were lonely for company.

In those days, guest rooms were stocked with the best linens, grandmother's quilts, and feather mattresses. Though the world is changing, human nature still has the same desire to please. Guests might be offered antique plates full of chocolate chip cookies, crystal carafes and glasses for mineral water, cut flowers, compact-disc alarms that glow-in-the-dark, and remote-control televisions.

As if all that were not enough to welcome guests, Americans often lavish rooms with even more extravagances in anticipation of their guests' every need. The visitors can take their pick of everything from down-filled pillows—soft or firm—in various shapes and sizes to just-released books and recent magazines. Good lighting is provided for reading. Also on hand are telephones, notepads and pencils, tissue boxes, and fabric boxes that are perfect for holding jewelry and watches.

Aside from spots for reading, writing, and putting one's feet up, rooms are outfitted with places for unpacking luggage. Though it takes a bit of planning, wallpapered closets host big fluffy robes on wooden hangers, and old chests offer nothing but empty drawers. Full-length mirrors hang on the backs of doors.

Since comfort is key, Americans like to offer guests the kind of plush overnight accommodations that they would expect

The restful shades of crimson and cognac help reinvent rosettes pulled from the rose-strewn coverlet. Self-ties keep flowers in place. Contrasting ties secure reversible bed hangings.

to find at the Hôtel Plaza Athénée, Hôtel Ritz, or Hôtel de Crillion in Paris. For putting cares to rest without princely prices, king beds—a rarity in grand Parisian hotels—are better than queens that top full-size beds and that are still better than twins. Regardless of size, when guests call, the best-dressed beds are worthy of the setting with beautiful, freshly pressed, high-thread-count linens, extra blankets, and *matelassé*—meaning padded or quilted—blanket covers.

For a long time now, designers have been suggesting that spending a night in one's guest room is a good test for it. After spending the night there, the room's shortcomings may become apparent.

✤ CHILDREN'S ROOMS ✤

Children, like adults, need their own space. The space does not have to be big and elaborate for them to feel special, just someplace that is their own where they can be themselves. Psychologists have said that children are happiest in bright, colorful, light rooms designed for their needs.

Regardless, many parents stop decorating at their children's bedroom doors, fearing they won't get long-term value for

If a trip to Paris is not in one's travel plans, escaping to this guest room might be almost as nice. With bold clean lines, the refined polished steel canopy bed became a classic after being introduced by the French around 1760. The tea-washed Bennison floral, from an early document, is artfully fashioned so it appears to have aged over time. Reflecting the spirit of relaxed living, nineteenth-century confit pots—now lamps—side a king-sized bed luxuriously plumped with pillows.

*W*hether five, ten, or fifteen years old, these fresh fabrics would fittingly outfit any girl's room. When major furnishings suit most ages, all it takes is a sisal rug and moving some accessories in or out to give a room the appropriate magic. Of course, small details help, too. Among those here are narrow contrasting welts edging the curtains, a cleverly constructed bed skirt, and a matelassé bedcover separating the mattress and boxsprings. Old picture frames are painted white.

Summer Hill fabrics and wallcovering meet at the top of this window treatment. White puff pique quilted on the diagonal in parallel double rows that carefully follow the lines of the fabric create the look shown here.

their money—and no wonder. A nursery often has a life span of a mere few years, so it makes sense to pass up the farm-animal motifs because children quickly outgrow them. Without question, an ideal room will grow with the child, which makes designing these pint-size spaces far from easy, considering the numerous ways they must function.

Beyond a place to rest one's precious head, a young child needs floor space for playing, creating, and stretching the imagination. For school-age children a spot for reading is also a necessity. Of course, growing up isn't hard to do in a room with a desk or worktable, a chair, a chest of drawers, and good light. The problem is, it isn't easy to come up with furnishings that will brave the bruises of childhood, smoothly make the transition into the teen years, then appropriately welcome the child back after he or she abandons the nest—while doubling as a guest room.

Consequently, many parents assume that just because they have spent a lot of time pulling together their children's rooms doesn't mean their children will take any better care of them. However, the truth is, children are more apt to keep up a space charted carefully, especially when they've helped with the planning.

Most of us are well schooled in the significance of a child's first five years of life, but importantly, in *The Decoration of Houses,* published more than 100 years ago, the late grand mistress of design, Edith Wharton, bluntly warned readers that threadbare nursery furnishings might forever thwart a child's developing good taste. Whether or not this is true, children obviously appreciate and may even thrive in well-planned appealing rooms.

✤ BATHROOMS ✤

The experts say most Americans spend seven years of their lives in the bathroom, where they relax, unwind, and pamper themselves in every way. Bathrooms are restoration spots where one goes to wake up under brass, chrome, or nickel-plated showerheads the size of the sun or to later relax in oversized cast-iron soaking tubs amidst bubbles. It is increasingly common these days for bathrooms to have space for exercise equipment, chaise lounges, and candles. Some new showers even include saunas and built-in television sets.

For their own reasons, Europeans lean toward timeless neutral bathrooms and place natural light near the top of their priority lists. In bathrooms lacking windows, they opt for skylights whenever possible, aware that a skylight emits more than triple the light that would come from a window the same size. Wall sconces flank mirrors, providing adequate light for applying makeup and shaving.

Unlike the French, most Americans do not have bidets installed in their bathrooms, but they do have a taste for the same beautifully textured, absorbent bath linens with the comfort of natural fibers, fine soaps, and enticing accessories commonly found in the French bath.

A symmetrical formal composition of imperial touches creates a seductive powder room, enhanced by various textures and accents of black and gold.

*ℬolts of soft flowing muslin create sweeping bed and window treatments as the more
sensuous hand-embroidered bed linens bring a hint of romance to everyday living.*

There is no better place for losing touch with the real world than in a freestanding, marble soaking tub— an antique that is complete with a bath rack. The handsome fittings are nickel.

An antique commode transformed into a vanity lords over a guest bath displaying the influence of Paris. Paintings, delicate linens, and a Louis XIV mirror—all worthy of the setting—give this guest bathroom a strong presence.

Dreams come alive in this charming room swathed in fabrics that mix well. Tom Kitten catches the morning sun. Later, a little girl will climb into her daddy's lap for a story. Lifting the bedroom ceiling allowed for the installation of an octagonal skylight with French paned windows and opaque glass.

All dressed up in decorative tile, this bathroom is as appropriate for today as tomorrow. The cotton mini-print embellishing the shades is one of the original Provence prints from Soleiado. Hand-painted cabinets with geranium pink accents add another feminine touch to a space shared by sisters.

A young boy's love for fishing with his dad offered endless inspiration for this room that looks as if it might be situated in the family's lake house. Bass, trout, and catfish wallcovering stream through old signs, photographs, a fish basket, and vintage rods.

A room with the charm of a painted French cottage or stone farmhouse is an ideal setting for the tall narrow cupboards flanking the daybed. During the French Revolution, soldiers hid in these cabinets with false drawers appropriately named homme, or man, and debout, or standing. Those shown here were custom-crafted for the designer.

All that is missing here is the baby. Later, when the parents welcome child number two, their firstborn will move into the room next door, and this room will remain the nursery.

For inspiration the soon-to-be parents studied children's books. Then the walls were readied for baby.

In days to come, this daybed will encourage a concerned parent to spend the night. For now, an eclectic mix of pillows tumbles about, brightening the room. The looming picture frame awaits baby.

𝒞voking all the charm of an old-fashioned sleeping porch, the imaginative Anna French wallcovering sets the palette for this room. The quilts gracing the white wicker beds are vintage, so are the hats. A sea-grass rug contributes to the Galveston Island, Carmel, or Nantucket mood. Propped on the glazed-lava table that was crafted in France is a painting by the young girl who lives in the home.

A delicately painted lamp, vintage wicker desk, and chair finished in a peeling blue paint brighten a corner. The matchstick blinds dressed in a cotton check and double bows invite in both the view and the light.

Toiles came to the United States after the American Revolution and remain popular today, but Americans still use them more sparingly than the French. Americans commonly incorporate solids, stripes, and checks with flair. The key to the deft blending of these fabrics is staying within one colorway. A toile will team with both checks and stripes in the same color family.

This guest room takes an innocent turn with the introduction of crisp white crib linens banded in red. A century ago, the Pratesi family began making beautiful linens for the Italian aristocracy. Before the nineteenth century, bedrooms were rarely found in the rural homes. According to Porthault, the renowned French linen house, one of the earliest orders for monogrammed linens came from Charles V in 1380.

In France, the alluring red-and-white toile might be this guest room's only fabric, but the designer put together a sophisticated American look, mixing the Pierre Deux toile with a Brunschwig & Fils plaid and mini-patterned sheer and piles of pillows. The stunning lit à baldaquin—canopy bed—defines French style. Yet, it is the small painted table built by the designer's father that gives this setting its charm. It offsets the formality of the room while instilling harmony.

Classical lines and subtle color create sedate splendor. To help special guests rest easy, softly gathered fan-pleated curtains echo the bed's sumptuous fabrics while strié wallcovering serves as a calm backdrop. When ordering wallpaper, one need keep in mind that European rolls measure twenty inches wide and eleven yards long, covering approximately fifty-five square feet. American rolls are twenty-seven inches wide and five yards long, covering thirty-three square feet.

Crafted in San Francisco by Shannon and Jeal, these polished-steel luggage racks are handsome enough to leave out between guests.

Happy Mothers Day

*O*n a plain white saucer, a talented San Francisco artist hand-painted a true-to-scale interpretation of the Provençal Travers print used in the room. Afterwards, the Houston designer affixed the fixture to the ceiling in her little girl's room.

❖

*H*appiness comes in shades of yellow, red, and pink that make growing up fun. A folding screen covered in the same medium-scaled print as the window panels is perfect for crowding favorite photographs and important artwork. It also serves as a portable wall and secret entrance to the doll room behind. An unpretentious sea-grass rug adds texture.

When one's mother is a designer, it is hardly surprising that she would put her creative talent to work plan-ning a mélange of pretty pillows, including one shaped like a handbag, nor is it unusual that she would res-cue the bench shown here from a flea market, knowing it would be ideal for dressing dolls and looking at books. The little girl who rests her pretty head here is also fond of ladybugs. The one on the floor was a gift from her Nana.

Obviously, some royal treatment was in order when it came to furnishing this little girl's room. Charming linens flatter the Jane Keltner hand-painted bed. Lengths of soft Provençal cotton print, lined and interlined, slide down smocked stationary panels. Smocked dotted sheers, mirroring the scale of the dots in the Osborne & Little wallcovering, provide privacy.

Is it any wonder that our fascination for France and all it represents has long been with us? It is not just that the French bring style and sophistication to everything they do or that their attention to detail defines

French ACCENTS

good taste, nor is it the passion that they bring to their personal space, making their architecturally and culturally rich country an even more strikingly beautiful place to live. Rather, it is all of these things. Their example of combining the ordinary with the extraordinary is inspiring. ❧ As the French carefully carve out comfortable spaces for themselves with unparalleled flair, they are able to see beauty in the simple things that are extensions of their lives. Whether it is Grandmère's antique linens, Aunt Stéphanie's pewter

Every house needs a quiet spot for reading a book, listening to music, or working a puzzle—enjoying life's simplest pleasures away from the pressures of the world. The joy of playing Candyland, Scrabble, or bridge can be savored at length at this table. In France, chic homes have stacks of books in every room.

*W*ith a nod to chinoiserie, fabric acts as a backdrop for clusters of opaline. Highly prized since the Middle Ages, opaline is of French origin with a translucent finish that reflects light. Often milky white, though frequently colored, it quietly sits atop a commode, waiting to be admired.

Tapestries have long played an important role in French interiors. This hand-woven eighteenth-century treasure adds a classic European touch to a grand entry. Suspended from an iron bar, it hangs on stenciled walls.

candlesticks, or a simple cachepot a mother passed down to her daughter—the size, the shape, or value is irrelevant, so long as the possessions in one's care tie together a family history. Because these treasures tell a story, they bring happiness, and the French cherish them.

Beyond family, friends, and France, itself, collecting seems to be what the French love most. As a result, they can extract the most commonplace items from daily life—old jars, jugs, books—and convert them into almost charming works of art simply by where they put them or the way they arrange them in their homes, but then, Americans can, too.

✤　　M I R R O R S　　✤

The mirror became the most sought-after symbol of French splendor when Louis XIV, smitten with his own reflection, decreed the construction of the Hall of Mirrors in the Palace of Versailles in 1678. Today, elegant mirrors still adorn some of the grander rooms in both town and country homes, but they are no longer simply looking glasses, as they were called until about 1875, designed for self-admiration. Rather than reflecting the vanity of society, they are useful for cleverly adding depth and dimension to rooms.

Strategically placed, generously sized mirrors make spaces look roomier than they are. Whether a reproduction or an antique, a mirror should be artfully hung where it reflects both light and something interesting, rather than a blank wall. The best strategy for creating the impression of ample space is to reflect the view from a window.

In the United States, there is a lingering impulse among some people to install an entire wall of mirrors. The French prefer elegantly framed mirrors that hang freely, mostly because they have more character and are more interestingly shaped.

The old-world charm of Paris makes its famous flea markets one of the best places to turn up chunky decanters and other interesting glassware.

Elegant cherry paneling heralds a love for horses and interest in racing. Lending easy sophistication to a regal library filled with memorabilia is a welcoming winged chair and a leather sofa mellowed by time.

The French government is highly protective of its vineyards, which are considered part of the national legacy. Ordinances prohibit foreign buyers from purchasing these properties without government approval. Frenchman Bruno de la Croix-Vaubois, who owns Country French Interiors in Dallas, Texas, sells the vintage wine jugs shown here.

This lamp, made of tin molds, brings both light and laughter to a kitchen.

*W*hen one designer could not find a laundry-room paper that ran horizontally to increase the feeling of space, she sketched her own. Then manufacturer Peter Fasano in Great Barrington, Massachusetts, stepped in, producing the "Clothes Line" shown here. Today it is in his collection at showrooms throughout the country.

In the sixteenth century, French nuns began painting and decorating metal and tin trays and boxes, an art that soon was known as "tôle." Here, vintage trays decorate a dining-room wall until called into service.

A pine table offers display space for a collection of blue-and-white Chinese pots, birds, and wall brackets. Hong Kong's return to China has sparked increased interest in the Far East and its decorative arts.

For centuries, blue has been a favored color. Here, layers of blue tie together a sumptuous living room accented with broad strokes of white. On a small antique table lies part of a collection of lapis animals. The chair fabric is Andre Bon. The paisley on the windows is from Clarence House.

In France, the backyard is the focal point of most homes. Doors fling open to attractive planters and urns spilling over with foliage. Well-planned exterior grounds flow from distinctive interiors with color

Outside INTERESTS

swatches effortlessly connecting both worlds. From the lush lawns where families dine and entertain *al fresco* in mild weather to the courtyards where birds sing to the unpretentious gardens, vegetation is carefully chosen. ⚜ Fruit trees share property rights with clusters of flowers, providing homegrown produce and bouquets. Sanded allées neatly outline *potagers*, or walled kitchen gardens, seeded with vegetables and herbs, communicating a love for cooking. ⚜ Plantings change, depending upon the soil and the

Topiary trees have been the mainstay of formal European gardens since the sixteenth century. Here, they trim white-and-green Italian pottery, and mirror the fanciful grape centerpiece awaiting luncheon guests. Hand-painted table linens complement the flowers in beds.

A pocket of tulips pushes through the soil in a peaceful spot away from the pressures of the world. The picnic basket, tablecloth, and napkins are from Williams-Sonoma.

climate. In Provence, splashes of lavender have grown since ancient times when it was used to scent bathwater. Today, it is used in everything from medicine to soap to potpourri, and for everything from repelling moths from closets to restoring peace of mind.

Shaded by ancient trees, painted wrought-iron and perforated tables, evoking the street cafés in postwar Paris, capture the spirit of France. Borrowing from this garden of ideas, we transport the ambiance of France to the United States, where settings satisfy the lifestyles, tastes, and wishes of citizens.

$\mathscr{W}$hat prettier place to enjoy lunch than on a stone wall in this garden? Unpretentious daffodils brighten the day, while a Hermès scarf serves as a tablecloth. Charger and painter's palette china are both from Limoges, France.

Sheer artistry defines spaces. Sophisticated white flowers and neatly trimmed bushes fuse with the land, framing the terraced gardens overlooking San Francisco.

*L*ush plants surround the gazebo, which is the perfect gathering place for family and friends, but even billowing with roses, it has competition for attention from both the pond and this gracefully landscaped yard.

*W*ith its easy-living decor, this pool house is a favorite destination that caters informally to family and friends. Low-maintenance terra-cotta tile readily handles spills. A wall of photographs chronicles lives much like a family album, while the vaulted ceiling creates the feeling of spaciousness without reducing the room's charm. Though this is a balmy beach house with a series of rooms, it could easily be a family room anywhere grounds are lush with bougainvillea.

An artfully executed loggia that opens to the outdoors is the perfect place for sharing laughs while catching a breath of fresh air. Indoor/outdoor curtains blur hard edges without disrupting the view. A generously scaled limestone fireplace offers warmth on chilly days. Regardless of the weather, the family's West Highland terrier enjoys the comforts of the room.

Fragrant pink and blue hyacinths are having their moment in the sun as the popularity of outdoor flower gardening continues to grow. The china is Ceraline from France.

In spring, the gate opens to a lawn covered with daffodils, crocuses, and hyacinths, then tulips, while large pots of ivy geraniums vie for rights to the terrace.

Adding decorative trim to window treatments, upholstered pieces, table skirts, and pillows is an easy way to give them character. The trims shown here are from Ellen Holt in Dallas.

Shopping for the home in France can be frustrating since the lengthy *pose midi* means almost everything is closed between noon and three o'clock in the afternoon. Also, many antique shops are closed early in the week. No matter—American designers generally rely on a select group of resources right here in the United States.

Trade Secrets

Of course, we often choose fabrics, furnishings, and fixtures from showrooms that are available "to the trade only." However, many of the accessories seen in this book are from well-known department stores such as Neiman Marcus, Bergdorf Goodman, Barneys New York, Bloomingdale's, and Saks Fifth Avenue. Another appealing retail establishment is Ralph Lauren. Additionally, it is not uncommon for us to look to Crate & Barrel, Pier 1, Pottery Barn, Williams-Sonoma, and Banana Republic, and we are big believers in catalog shopping, too, especially Ballard Designs and Horchow. Here are a few more places we feel are worth a special look.

ATLANTA, GEORGIA

Boxwoods Gardens & Gifts
100 East Andrews Drive
Atlanta, GA 30305
404-233-3400
*One-of-a-kind gifts, antiques,
plants*

Pierre Deux
3500 Peachtree Road N.E.
Atlanta, GA 30326
404-869-7790
*French-country antiques, home
furnishings, fabrics*

The Gables
711 Miami Circle
Atlanta, GA 30324
404-231-0734
800-753-3342
*Eighteenth- and nineteenth-
century French-country
furniture, accessories*

Glyn Weakley, Ltd.
3489 Northside Parkway
N.W.
Atlanta, GA 30327
404-841-6649
Distinctive accessories, gifts

Jeff Jones Designs
2101 A Tula Street
(at Bennett Street)
Atlanta, GA 30309
404-350-0711
*Architectural items, antiques,
chandeliers, rugs, furniture*

The Plantation Shop
96 East Andrews Drive
Atlanta, GA 30305
404-841-0065
*French and English antiques,
china, home furnishings*

Travis Interiors
12 Kings Circle N.E.
Atlanta, GA 30305
404-233-7207
Antiques, pillows

BOSTON, MASSACHUSETTS

Autrefois
125 Newbury Street
Boston, MA 02116
617-424-8823
French antiques

Camden Companies, Inc.
211 Berkeley Street
Boston, MA 02116
617-421-9899
*Painted furniture, antiques,
pillows, bedcovers*

Pierre Deux
111 Newbury Street
Boston, MA 02116
617-536-6364
*French-country antiques
and home furnishings, fabrics*

Industry
276 Newbury Street
Boston, MA 02116
617-437-0319
*Painted wares by local artists,
including tables, lampshades*

La Ruche
168 Newbury Street
Boston, MA 02116
617-536-6366
*Decorative accessories
for home and garden*

Marcoz Antiques
177 Newbury Street
Boston, MA 02116
617-262-0780
*Whimsical antiques
and accessories, china*

Upstairs Downstairs
93 Charles Street
Boston, MA 02114
617-367-1950
*Home and garden furniture,
silver, accessories*

CHARLOTTE, NORTH CAROLINA

Bedside Manor
6822-E Phillip's Place Court
Charlotte, NC 28210
704-554-7727
*Bed and bath, linens, antique
beds, hostess gifts*

Charlotte's Garden
715 Providence Road
Charlotte, NC 28207
704-333-5353
*Garden furniture, trellises,
botanical pillows, French tin
buckets*

Circa
2321 Crescent Avenue
Charlotte, NC 28207
704-332-1668
Home furnishings and antiques

The English Room
519 Fenton Place
Charlotte, NC 28207
704-377-3625
Antiques, paintings, accessories

Jenko's
715 Providence Road
Charlotte, NC 28207
704-375-1779
*French and English antiques,
accessories, hand-painted
pillows*

Queen Charlotte
Antiques, Ltd.
603 Providence Road
Charlotte, NC 28207
704-333-0472
*Eighteenth- and nineteenth-
century French furniture,
light fixtures, paintings*

CHICAGO, ILLINOIS

Mike Bell
1869 Merchandise Mart
Chicago, IL 60654
312-644-6848
Antiques and reproductions

Belvedere
948 Rush Street
Chicago, IL 60611
312-664-4200
*Tabletops, modern and antique
designs*

Pierre Deux
996 Green Bay Road
Winnetka, IL 60093
847-441-7755
*French-country antiques and
home furnishings, fabrics*

Thomas R. Jolly, Inc.
220 West Kinzie Street
Fifth Floor
Chicago, IL 60616
312-595-0018
Antiques

La Maison De Nicole
66 East Walton
Chicago, IL 60611
312-943-3988
Tabletops

A New Leaf
1645 North Wells Street
Chicago, IL 60614
312-642-1576
*Accessories, collectibles,
    garden items*

DALLAS, TEXAS

Amen Wardy Home
42 Highland Park Village
Dallas, TX 75205
214-522-6763
*Home furnishings and
    accessories*

Country French Interiors
1428 Slocum Street
Dallas, TX 75207
214-747-4700
*Eighteenth- and nineteenth-
    century French-country
    furniture, accessories*

Pierre Deux
415 Decorative Center
Dallas, TX 75207
214-749-7775
*French-country antiques and
    home furnishings, fabrics*

It's A Wrap
25 Highland Park
    Shopping Village
Dallas, TX 75205
214-520-9727
*Accessories, invitations,
    gift wrapping*

Lady Primrose
500 Crescent Court
Dallas, TX 75201
214-871-8333
    *Antiques, accessories,
bath products, tea room*

The Mews
1708 Market Center
    Boulevard (at Oak Lawn)
Dallas, TX 75207
214-748-9070
Stable of antique shops

Rolston & Bonick
Antiques for the Garden
2905 North Henderson
Dallas, TX 75206
214-826-7775
Garden ornaments

Room Service
4354 Lovers Lane
Dallas, TX 75225
214-369-7666
Accessories and gifts

Rutherford's
5647 West Lovers Lane
Dallas, TX 75209
214-357-0888
*Fabrics, trims, accessories,
    including pillows and lamps*

Trumeau of Dallas
2800 Routh Street
Dallas, TX 75201
214-871-1171
Accessories and gifts

Uncommon Market, Inc.
2701 Fairmount
Dallas, TX 75201
214-871-2775
*Antiques, French iron lighting,
accessories, leather-bound books*

HOUSTON, TEXAS

Area
3200 Shepherd
Houston, TX 77098
713-528-0220
*Antiques and accessories,
    including mirrors*

Events
1966 West Gray
Houston, TX 77019
713-520-5700
*Accessories, tabletop,
    one-of-a-kind items*

Joyce Horn Antiques
1022 Witt Road, #316
Houston, TX 77055
713-688-0507
*French farm tables, bird cages,
    paintings*

Kay O'Toole Antiques
    and Eccentricities
1921 Westheimer
Houston, TX 77027
713-621-4404
Antiques and accessories

Krispen Antiques
3723 Westheimer
Houston, TX 77027
*Furniture, pottery, paintings,
    and a garden shop*

Longoria Collection
6524 Woodway
Houston, TX 77057
713-467-8495
*Linens, furniture,
    and accessories*

Made in France
2912 Ferndale Place
Houston, TX 77098
713-529-7949
Antiques and accessories

Maison Maison
1608 Bissonnet
Houston, TX 77005
713-520-7426
Accessories, pillows

The Mews
5120 Woodway, Suite 107
Houston, TX 77056
713-621-9112
Antiques and accessories

Carl Moore Antiques
1610 Bissonnet
Houston, TX 77005
713-524-2502
French-country antiques

Jane Moore Interiors
2922 Virginia
Houston, TX 77098
713-526-6113
Antiques and accessories

Brian Stringer Antiques
2031 West Alabama
Houston, TX 77098
713-526-7380
*Antiques, reproductions from
    France, England, and Italy*

Watkins, Schatte & Culver
    Antiques
2308 Bissonnet
Houston, TX 77005
713-529-0597
*Hand-painted furnishings from
    Provence, old chandeliers,
    and mantels*

**LOS ANGELES,
CALIFORNIA**

Algabar
920 North La Cienega
    Boulevard
Los Angeles, CA 90069
310-360-3500
*Furniture, French birdcages,
    antique accessories*

Brenda Antin
7319 Beverly Boulevard
Los Angeles, CA 90036
213-934-8451
*Antique sleigh beds,
    fabrics, and tapestries*

The Blue House
8440 Melrose Avenue
Los Angeles, CA 90069
213-852-0747
Unique French antiques

NASHVILLE, TENNESSEE

Bella Linea
6031 Highway 100
    (in West Gate Center)
Nashville, TN 37205
615-352-4041
*Nineteenth-century iron beds,
    linens*

Made in France
3001 West End Avenue
Nashville, TN 37203
615-329-9300
*Old and new iron furniture,
    architectural pieces,
    accessories*

Street Smart
2416 Elliston Place
Nashville, TN 37203
615-329-9337
*Hand-painted pottery,
    accessories, gifts*

The Tulip Tree
6025 Highway 100
    (in West Gate Center)
Nashville, TN 37205
615-352-1466
*Garden accessories,
    custom-designed tablecloths*

NEW ORLEANS, LOUISIANA

Angèle Parlange Design
5419 Magazine Street
New Orleans, LA 70115
504-897-6511
*Hand-painted fabrics,
    furnishings for bed and bath*

Bremermann Designs
3943 Magazine Street
New Orleans, LA 70115
504-891-7763
Antiques

Bush Antiques
2109 Magazine Street
New Orleans, LA 70130
504-581-3518
*Eclectic French furniture and
    antiques*

Dixon & Dixon of Royal
237–239 Royal Street
    and 319 Chartres Street
New Orleans, LA 70130
504-524-0282
800-848-5148
*Eighteenth- and nineteenth-
    century French-country
    furniture, rugs, paintings,
    antiques*

Lucullus
610 Chartres Street
New Orleans, LA 70130
504-528-9620
Culinary antiques

Regency House Antiques
841 Royal Street
New Orleans, LA 70116
504-524-7507
French and English antiques

Shop of the Two Sisters
1800 Magazine Street
New Orleans, LA 70130
Collectibles

Wirthmore
3727, 3900, and 5723
    Magazine Street
New Orleans, LA 70115
504-897-9727
504-899-3811
*Eighteenth- and nineteenth-
    century French-country
    antiques*

NEW YORK, NEW YORK

NEW YORK— UPPER EAST SIDE

Didier Aaron
32 East 67th Street
    (Madison at Park)
New York, NY 10021
212-988-5248
*Eclectic European furniture,
    paintings, drawings*

E. Braun & Co.
717 Madison Avenue
    (between 63rd and 64th)
New York, NY 10021
212-838-0650
*Linens, custom embroidery
    to match china and wall
    coverings*

Yale R. Burge
315 East 62nd Street
New York, NY 10021
212-838-4005
*Antique French furniture,
    reproductions, accessories*

Pierre Deux
870 Madison Avenue
    (at 71st)
New York, NY 10021
212-570-9343
*French-country antiques and
    home furnishings, fabrics*

En Soie
988 Madison Avenue
    (at 77th)
New York, NY 10021
212-717-7958
*Furniture, fabrics, pillows,
    hand-painted ceramics*

Elizabeth Street Garden
    & Gallery
1176 Second Avenue
    (at 62nd)
New York, NY 10021
212-644-6969
*Antique garden ornaments,
    stone urns, benches*

Gazebo of New York
114 East 57th Street
    (between Park and
    Lexington)
New York, NY 10021
212-832-7077
*Quilts, rugs, pillows, and
    accessories*

Léron Linens
750 Madison Avenue
    (at 65th)
New York, NY 10021
212-249-3188
European linens

Lexington Gardens
1011 Lexington Avenue
    (between 72nd and 73rd)
New York, NY 10021
212-861-4390
*Antiques and garden-inspired
    furnishings*

Adrien Linford
927 Madison Avenue
    (at 74th)
New York, NY 10021
212-628-4500
*Books, painted pottery,
    glassware*

Mèlonie de France
41 East 60th Street
New York, NY 10022
212-935-4343
Harmonious blend of antiques

Mackenzie-Childs, Ltd.
824 Madison Avenue
    (at 69th)
New York, NY 10021
212-570-6050
Furniture, glassware,
    candle shades, tiles

Ronaldo Maia
27 East 67th Street
    (between Park & Madison)
New York, NY 10021
212-288-1049
Topiaries, vases, candles

Slatkin & Co.
131 East 70th Street
    (between Park &
    Lexington)
New York, NY 10021
212-794-1661
Antique ceramics, toiles

Solanée
866 Lexington Avenue
    (at 65th)
New York, NY 10021
212-439-6109
800-717-6526
Tableware and glassware
    from France

Trelliage
418 East 75th Street
New York, NY 10021
212-535-2288
Garden furniture and antique
    accessories

Karen Warshaw, Ltd.
167 East 74th Street
    (Lexington at Third)
New York, NY 10021
212-439-7870
French and English antiques
    and paintings

NEW YORK—MIDTOWN

ABC Carpet & Home
888 Broadway
    (at 19th)
New York, NY 10003
212-473-3000
French linens, oriental rugs,
    antiques, furniture, and
    accessories

Hyman Hendler & Sons
67 West 38th Street
New York, NY 10018
212-840-8393
Ribbons for upholstery

MJ Trimmings
1008 Avenue of the Americas
New York, NY 10018
212-391-9072 and
212-764-5854
Tassels, cords, braids, and
    buttons

NEW YORK— GREENWICH VILLAGE

Pierre Deux Antiques
369 Bleecker Street
    (at Charles)
New York, NY 10014
212-243-7740
French-country furniture
    and accessories

NEW YORK—SOHO

Intérieurs
114 Wooster Street
New York, NY 10012
212-343-0800
Tables from south of France,
    accessories

Nanz Custom Hardware
20 Vandam Street
New York, NY 10013
212-367-7000
Hardware

Wolfman-Gold & Good Co.
117 Mercer Street
    (between Prince & Spring)
New York, NY 10012
212-966-7055
Tabletop, ceramics

Zona
97 Green Street
    (between Prince & Spring)
New York, NY 10012
212-925-6750
Chenille throws, antique
    garden tools

SAN DIEGO, CALIFORNIA

Circa A.D.
3867 Fourth Avenue
San Diego, CA 92103
619-293-3328
Garden ornaments

Maison en Provence
820 Ford Stockton Drive
San Diego, CA 92103
619-298-5318
Home furnishings from France

Virtu
4416 Park Boulevard
San Diego, CA 92116
619-543-9150
Antiques and garden accessories

SAN FRANCISCO, CALIFORNIA

Pierre Deux
134 Maiden Lane
San Francisco, CA 94108
415-296-9940
French-country antiques and
    home furnishings, fabrics

Fillamento
2185 Fillmore Street
San Francisco, CA 94115
415-931-2224
Tabletop accessories, linens

Gump's
135 Post Street
San Francisco, CA 94108
415-982-1616
800-766-7628
Antiques, garden accessories,
    and linens

Hilary Thatz
38 Stanford Shopping Center
Palo Alto, CA 94304
650-323-4200
French-country furniture, acces-
    sories, paintings, tabletop

Intérieur Perdu
340 Bryant Street
San Francisco, CA 94107
415-543-1616
Wrought-iron beds, bistro
    chairs, enamel kitchenware
    from France

Sue Fisher King
3067 Sacramento Street
San Francisco, CA 94115
415-922-7276
Linens, china, silver,
    garden accessories

Directory of Interior Designers and Firms

Diane Chapman
Diane Chapman Interiors
3380 Washington Street
San Francisco, CA 94118
415-346-2373
Fax: 415-346-5264

Cheryl Driver
Hilary Thatz
38 Stanford Shopping Center
Palo Alto, CA 94304
650-323-4200
Fax: 650-323-8300

Charles Faudree
Charles Faudree, Inc.
1314 East 15th Street
Tulsa, OK 74120
918-747-9706
Fax: 918-583-2380

Bruce Foreman, ASID
Bruce Givens Foreman
& Associates, Inc.
6262 Highland Road
Baton Rouge, LA 70808
504-769-3745
Fax: 504-767-1356

Muriel Hebert
Muriel Hebert Interiors
117 Sheridan Road
Piedmont, CA 94110
510-547-1294
Fax: 510-655-1509

Katherine Hill
Katherine Hill Interiors
3436 Clay Street
San Francisco, CA 94118
415-922-6055
Fax: 415-351-2625

Janet Hodges and Amy Young
Hodges and Young Design
3912 Lenox Drive
Fort Worth, TX 76107
817-737-8575
Fax: 817-877-5606

Gloria Nicoud, ASID
Gloria Designs
4237 Arcady Avenue
Dallas, TX 75205
214-526-5912
Fax: 214-526-2074

Constance Noah
Constance Noah Interior
Design
2019 Soledad Avenue
La Jolla, CA 92037
619-459-7051
Fax: 619-459-0046

Betty Lou Phillips, ASID
and IIDA
Interiors by BLP
4278 Bordeaux Avenue
Dallas, TX 75205
214-599-0191
Fax: 214-599-0192

Christina Phillips, ASID
CMP Designs
5001 River Bluff Drive
Fort Worth, TX 76132
817-292-3994
Fax: 817-292-3694

Marilyn Phillips
Loren Interiors
1125 River Bend Drive
Houston, TX 77063
713-973-6475
Fax: 713-973-8859

Tellingly, this designer is passionate about symmetry and relentless in the pursuit of perfection. Obviously, he is also partial to dogs.

Richard Trimble, ASID
Richard Trimble &
Associates, Inc.
6517 Hillcrest Road, #318
Dallas, TX 75205
214-363-2283
Fax: 214-363-6364

Chris Van Wyk
Chris Van Wyk Designs
75 Westover Terrace
Fort Worth, TX 76107
817-735-9400
Fax: 817-735-4747

Danica Woody
McKay's Interiors
17820 Sotile Drive
Baton Rouge, LA 70809
504-752-1841
Fax: 504-752-1982

❖

PHOTOGRAPHIC CREDITS

All photographs for this book are by Daniel Piassick for Colleen Duffley Studio except for the following, which appear with permission: Colleen Duffley—pages v, viii, 13, 55, 105, 106; Janet Lenzen—page 49; David Livingston—pages 21, 24, 99; Russell McMasters—page 22; Jon Jensen pages—36, 74, 75; courtesy Country Floors—pages 67 bottom, 78, 79; courtesy Meredith Corporation—pages 36, 74, 75; courtesy Color Wheel Company—page 9.

DESIGNER CREDITS

The room designs of the following interior designers appear on pages as noted: Charles Faudree—pages 28, 35, 40, 46, 56, 68, 107, 129, 149; Marilyn Phillips—pages 43, 49, 67 top, 80, 114, 115, 121, 122, 123, 132; Cheryl Driver—pages 22, 24, 59, 77, 99, 108, 109, 111; Richard Trimble—pages 5, 33, 54, 57, 62, 65, 71, 76 bottom, 93, 127, 128, 133 left, 141, 143, 151; Gloria Nicoud—pages ii, 32, 58, 60 bottom, 61, 86, 88, 89; Chris Van Wyk—pages v, viii, 13, 55, 105, 106; Betty Lou Phillips—pages vi, x, 6, 8, 12, 16, 20, 23, 25, 30, 36, 38, 52, 53, 64, 74, 75, 84, 85, 90, 91, 94, 96, 97, 100, 101, 102, 103, 118, 119, 130, 131, 134, 136, 137, 142; Bruce Foreman—pages 81, 92, 124; Muriel Hebert—pages 2, 72, 73, 104, 116, 117, 126, 133 right, 138, 139; Constance Noah—pages 26, 29, 82, 83, 140; Danica Woody—pages 10, 37, 87; Christina Phillips—pages 19, 110; Janet Hodges and Amy Young—pages 112, 113; Diane Chapman and Katherine Hill—page 21.

ARCHITECTURE CREDITS

D. C. Broadstone, Dallas, Texas—page x; A. Hays Town, Baton Rouge, Louisiana—page 3; Richardson Robertson, Los Angeles, California—page v.

❖